Going to the Tigers

WRITERS ON WRITING
Jay Parini, Series Editor

A good writer is first a good reader. Looking at craft from the inside, with an intimate knowledge of its range and possibilities, writers also make some of our most insightful critics. With this series we will bring together the work of some of our finest writers on the subject they know best, discussing their own work and that of others, as well as concentrating on craft and other aspects of the writer's world.

Poet, novelist, biographer, and critic, Jay Parini is the author of numerous books, including *The Apprentice Lover* and *One Matchless Time: A Life of William Faulkner*. Currently he is D. E. Axinn Professor of English & Creative Writing at Middlebury College.

Going to the Tigers

Essays and Exhortations

❧

Robert Cohen

University of Michigan Press
Ann Arbor

For questions or permissions, please contact um.press.perms@umich.edu

Published in the United States of America by the
University of Michigan Press
Printed and bound by CPI Group (UK) Ltd, Croydon, CR0 4YY

First published August 2022

A CIP catalog record for this book is available from the British Library.

Library of Congress Cataloging-in-Publication Data

Names: Cohen, Robert, 1957- author. | Michigan Publishing (University of Michigan),
    publisher.
Title: Going to the tigers : essays and exhortations / Robert Cohen.
Other titles: Writers on writing (Ann Arbor, Mich.)
Description: Ann Arbor : University of Michigan Press, 2022. | Series: Writers on
    writing
Identifiers: LCCN 2022013683 (print) | LCCN 2022013684 (ebook) |
    ISBN 9780472075553 (hardcover) | ISBN 9780472055555 (paperback) |
    ISBN 9780472220564 (ebook)
Subjects: LCSH: Authorship. | Creative writing. | English language—Style. | BISAC:
    LANGUAGE ARTS & DISCIPLINES / Writing / Fiction Writing | BIOGRAPHY
    & AUTOBIOGRAPHY / Personal Memoirs
Classification: LCC PN145 .C65 2022 (print) | LCC PN145 (ebook) | DDC 808.02—
    dc23/eng/20220510
LC record available at https://lccn.loc.gov/2022013683
LC ebook record available at https://lccn.loc.gov/2022013684

ALSO BY ROBERT COHEN

Amateur Barbarians
Inspired Sleep
The Varieties of Romantic Experience
The Here and Now
The Organ Builder
The Writer's Reader (co-editor)

Contents

Acknowledgments

Thanks are due to the editors and magazines where these essays, in one form or another, previously appeared: "Emblem, Essence," "Ain't That Pretty At All, or Going to the Tigers," and "Refer Madness" in *The Believer*; "The Piano Has Been Drinking" in *Georgia Review*; "Invisible Ink" in *Salmagundi*; "The Uncertainty Principle" in *Boulevard*; "Living, Loving, Temple-Going" in *Ninth Letter*; "A Maker of Mirrors" and "Kafka's Budget Guide to Florence" in *Paris Review Daily*; "Elkin" in *New England Review*; and "C. and Sardinia" in *The New York Times*.

The Uncertainty Principle

Some years back, in preparation for that ritualized dog-and-pony show, the academic job search, I was asked to give a talk. This seems fair enough in retrospect, but at the time it sounded ominous. For one thing I had no idea what a talk *was*. It was not that I had never given a talk before; I had never *gone* to a talk either. All I knew about talks was that they were not, properly speaking, talks at all, but rather hideously boring lectures on narrow, abstruse topics of a kind I'd made it more or less my goal in life never to attend.

Meanwhile the chair, sensing panic on my end of the phone, gently suggested a few options. I could discuss one or another literary principle I held dear. I could elucidate some particular issue of craft. Or if I preferred, I could do an old-fashioned close-reading, perform a detailed analysis of a "text."

In the silence that followed it became clear, to me anyway, that this academic job thing was not going my way. What business did I have applying for a job? I hated analyzing "texts," I rarely thought in terms of craft, and to the best of my knowledge I had no identifiable literary principles at all. Was I supposed to? Like most writers I avoided principled positions of any kind, and shared a fear of analysis that afflicts many pathological people: the fear that, to quote Donald Barthelme, "tear a mystery to tatters and you have tatters, not mystery."

Not that I said any of this to the chair of the English Department. What I said was, "Sure, fine, no problem." Then I headed out to my afternoon class.

Along the way I began to wonder whether I might indeed have some literary principles after all. And if so, was it possible that on some level I was actually communicating these principles to my students without being aware of it? When I arrived, I put the question to them. I said, Look, I have to go give a talk next week about my literary principles, and I have to sound vaguely intelligent and articulate on the subject and ideally even believe what I'm saying. So let me ask you guys: What do I talk about in here the most?

Death, they said.

What about second most?

Sex, they said.

Okay fine, I said. What about third most?

They hesitated. "Um . . ." they said at last, "uncertainty?"

Immediately I knew that they were right. That if the working life of a writer had taught me anything, had nurtured in me any pedagogical or aesthetic credo; that if I understood, in short, anything about writing—at least my own—for certain, it was that uncertainty was all. Knowledge in the material world may be power, but in the artistic sphere it's death.

The most common failing of novice fiction, I've come to believe, is neither a lack of talent or technical skill, nor an insufficient grounding in one's literary forebears, but rather a flawed and hasty empiricism that leads the writer to believe he/she knows something important about the world when much of the time he/she actually doesn't. Or rather they do know *some*thing. What they don't know, or often can't find a way to express, is *two* things—namely, that something and its opposite. And it's this two-ness, this promiscuous and paradoxical duality that it is both our nature and the world's, that provides the dynamic tension that makes art possible, and perhaps even necessary.

And yet what a strenuous process it is, to maintain this double vision, this split-screen perception. It's almost too much of a load to bear. It's like when you have a baby, and you suddenly look around you at the adults of the species, with their withered, misshapen bodies, their bad teeth and bad hair, their floppy sandals and baggy T-shirts, and you think: this perfectly adorable little dumpling, who's only about half a foot long, is going to turn into *that*? The prospect seems ludicrous, almost oxymoronic. But then so is reality ludicrous and oxymoronic. To comprehend its full paradoxical workings requires what Fitzgerald famously called the test of a first-rate intelligence: the ability to hold two opposing ideas in the mind at the same time and still be able to function.

Speaking personally, I fear I do not in fact possess a first-rate intelligence. Though I do have one important trait of a *second*-rate intelligence, which is the ability to appreciate a first-rate intelligence when it presents itself.

Take Tolstoy for example. There's a moment early in *War and Peace*, where in the midst of one of those lushly elaborate dinner parties he likes to throw for his characters, the writer allows his narrative gaze to glide around the room, as the butler does with his wine bottle, from Berg to Vera to Boris to Pierre to Natasha and at last, as a seeming afterthought, to the children's German tutor, a character we have to this point never met or even known existed. The tutor, a rather shy young man, sits there quietly at the table, watching the others:

> trying to remember all the dishes, wines, and kinds of dessert, in order to send a full description of the dinner to his people in Germany; and he felt greatly offended when the butler with a bottle passed him by. He frowned, trying to appear as if he did not want any of that wine, but was mortified because no one would understand that it was not to quench his thirst or from greediness that he wanted it, but simply from a conscientious desire for knowledge.

This odd little digressive foray into the consciousness of a character so minor as to scarcely even register—he's not even dignified with a name—is, I submit, one of the most profoundly beautiful moments in all of literature. So suddenly are we drawn into the longings and torments of a relatively "insignificant" person, and so movingly, that the white space that follows (the chapter ends there) goes on reverberating with it, reminding us that in the eyes of others we are all equally anonymous, earnest, and complex. We too are caught in Tolstoy's expansive web, enfolded in his omniscient grasp, pushed deeper below the surface and into the very heart of things—which is, as hearts are, multi-chambered.

Still, let's face it: most writers are not Tolstoy. (Some would say in real life—whatever *that* is—even Tolstoy wasn't Tolstoy). We may find, in reaching for that astonishingly capacious breadth and depth of vision, that it comes at the expense of the story itself, which for all its dazzling depths has mysteriously lost the ability to move forward. Strolling through the city of fiction, you can't stop and pay attention to everyone you pass, can't empty out your pockets for everyone in need. You'll be late for your appointments; you'll run out of money; you'll make impulsive, irrational, often ruthlessly arbitrary decisions about where to invest your spare quarters; in time you may decide to stop going out altogether. And then what?

No, for writers, idealists, and control freaks in general, it's the whimsical arbitrariness of these decisions—their near-weightless uncertainty—that proves, in the end, so threatening. I'm writing a story where I give X red hair, Y a brown shag, while Z, poor Z, is forced to go around in a mohawk. Or wait, maybe that's all wrong? The only way to find out if I'm right is to *make* myself right—to work through the possibilities of X, Y, and Z until they and their hairstyles are no longer floating in some zero-gravity space governed by sheer chance, but have become over the course of multiple drafts organically connected, as we used to say back in college. But isn't there some other, easier way?

The late Natalia Ginzburg, in her marvelous essay, "My Vocation," describes how in her early stories she would mark her characters:

> with some grotesque detail, and there was something nasty in this; I had a kind of malign resentment against reality. It was not a resentment based on anything real, because at that time I was a happy girl, but it appeared as a kind of reaction against naivete; it was that special resentment with which a naïve person who always thinks she being made a fool of defenders herself... irony and nastiness seemed to be very important weapons in my hands; I thought they would help me write like a man.

We all know by now what she means by that damning indictment: *write like a man*. She means a smug, privileged, tall-in-the-saddle, get-along-there-little-dogies air of control. She means the dumb, heedless authority of *knowing*. And yet if we examine the work of great writers who do happen to be men, what do we find? An odd tonal hybrid that often includes, for want of a better phrase, a kind of womanliness.

For a particularly vivid and unsettling example of this, consider Isaac Babel's "My First Goose." Like most Babel stories it's a deceptively straightforward account of a brainy young man's initiation into the hard, brutal world of the Cossack. Ridiculed by his fellows for his intellectual ways, his glasses, his apartness, his trunk full of manuscripts, the narrator thinks and broods. Finally, restless with hunger, he rouses himself to take action. First he punches his landlady in the chest; then he cracks the neck of a goose with the heel of his boot. (The goose, he tells us, had been "inoffensively preening his feathers" at the time). Naturally this sort of thing goes over like gangbusters with his new pals the Cossacks. "The lad's all right," they say, and invite him to share their meal. "What's in the newspaper?" they ask him. "Lenin writes," he reports, "that there's a shortage of everything." Afterwards they all lie down in the hayloft for the night, "warming one another, our legs intermingled. I dreamed, and in my dreams saw women. But my heart, stained with bloodshed, grated and brimmed over."

These final images of male-female entanglement send us back to the story's beginning, looking for clues. And lo, here they are, in the very first paragraph:

> Savitsky, Commander of the VI Division, rose when he saw me, and I wondered at the beauty of his giant's body. . . . A smell of scent and

the sickly-sweet freshness of soap emanated from him. His long legs were like girls sheathed to the neck in shining riding boots.

Later, after killing the goose and watching the landlady bear it off towards the kitchen—"Comrade," she tells him, "I want to go and hang myself"—he feels depressed, and looks up to see the moon hanging above the yard "like a cheap earring." The evening, he tells us, "laid a mother's hand upon my burning forehead." And so on. It's as if his adventure in male violence has paradoxically taken Babel's narrator (and presumably Babel himself) into a world of female sensitivities, female intuitions, female longings. But maybe that's too simple, too binary. It might be more accurate to say he has entered an imaginative sphere where such distinctions are no longer adequate, or even relevant; where male and female, aggressor and victim, Cossack and Jew, strength and weakness, all lie intermingled in one tortuously tangled, infinitely compromised self—the very self Babel's art embodied, if not embraced.

Or consider the good doctor Chekhov, a maestro of mixed moods and tones if there ever was one. Who can keep them straight? If there was ever a writer who denied us the comfort of knowing anything for certain, who forced us to question the testimony of every narrator, to second-guess every motive or intention, to see shadows of ambivalence, self-deception, and regret behind every action (or more frequently, non-action), it's the man who wrote:

> He had two lives, an open one, seen and known by all who needed to know it, full of conventional truth and conventional falsehood, exactly like the lives of his friends and acquaintances; and other life that went on in secret. And through some strange, perhaps accidental, combination of circumstances, everything that was of interest an importance to him, everything that was essential to him, everything about which he felt sincerely and did not deceive himself, everything that constituted the core of his life, was going on concealed from others . . . judging others by himself, he did not believe what he saw, and always fancied that every man led his real, most interesting life under cover of secrecy as under cover of night.

What makes Chekhov's work so sneaky and persuasive is his clinical impassivity, his refusal to supply answers or judgments, his unwillingness to reduce the emotional progression, if we can call it that, of his stories to an Either/Or dichotomy, one and not the other. With Chekhov it's always *two*-ness, always *Both/And*. When Anna Sergeyevna, the Lady with the

Pet Dog, lies to her husband about her rendezvous, he "did and did not believe her." If he believes her he's a dope, if he doesn't he's a cynic or a coward; either way he's that much more ripely deserving of cuckoldry. But if he both does and does not believe her at the same time? Then it's murky. Then it's difficult. Then he's like the rest of us—at once vaguely suspicious, vaguely hopeful, vaguely conflict-avoidant, and vaguely several other things too.

Chekhov offers his characters and readers no easy paths. Every blessing is mixed, every gift has a price tag. When Gurov arrives at the theater and sees the object of his obsession sitting in the crowd, his heart, the translation tells us, "contracts." Actually it's his *mind* that contracts; his heart, which has been underemployed to this point, *expands* at the sight of

> this little undistinguished woman, lost in a provincial crowd, with a vulgar lorgnette in her hand, filled his whole life now, was his sorrow and his joy, the only happiness that he now desired for himself, and to the sounds of the bad orchestra, of the miserable local violins, he thought how lovely she was. He thought and dreamed.

As in Babel, the movement from contraction to expansion—from a rational hierarchy of logic and taste to a chaos of sorrow and joy, from order and control to surrender and dreams—is anticipated symbolically beforehand, when upon his arrival at S___, Gurov finds on the table in his hotel room "an inkstand, gray with dust and topped by a figure on horseback, its hat in its raised hand and its head broken off." To find one's heart must one lose one's head? Maybe so. Certainly for a cold fish like Gurov, this by itself is a big step forward. But for Chekhov, who takes the aerial view, it may be not such a big step at all, as the heart by itself will not prevail either. In the tango of love and life, more than one organ is required. That's just realism. Messy quotidian truth. For all the wrenching disruptions Gurov and Anna have undertaken in the course of the story, all the tumult and lies that have upended their existence in pursuit of what seems, by the end, a fully mature affair, the last words of the story remind us they have only made a "beginning."

When fiction doesn't work, it's because it doesn't feel true. And it doesn't feel true because it advances one truth of existence but neglects its shadow, its hermeneutic twin. With Chekhov we enter a world of uncertainty, counterpoint, ambiguity, and find we're helpless to leave. We don't *want* to leave. To remain there is to nurture and flex some of our most useful literary muscles—our sense of patience, of negative capability; our capacity for *in*action and *ir*resolution; our willingness *not* to make up our minds, *not* to know what the hell we're saying or doing, *not* to close off the possibilities of a story but rather follow them deeper in, making of this tangled profusion our substance and fuel, indeed our very subject.

Of course, all this is easier said than done. Patience and negative capability are generally not the strong suits of your avid young writer bursting with ideas. They certainly weren't mine, back when I was young and avid and bursting with ideas.

Nowadays as it happens I am not bursting with ideas. Nowadays I rarely entertain ideas, and when I do they never arrive alone but in frazzled and contentious pairs, like couples on their way to a dinner party, debating whether to turn around and go home. That's just how my ideas behave these days, on those few occasions when I have them over. It's not clear why, but when someone calls to talk about some great new idea they have, I feel an irresistible urge to hang up the phone and lie down.

My view of ideas in fiction—my *idea*, I suppose, about ideas in fiction—is that they're only useful when they're at least half-useless, a kind of slapdash, slightly stoned intuition or glorified impression, more interesting than true. Then they can be *terrifically* useful. Writers like Dostoevsky and Mann, like Lawrence and Huxley, like Bellow and Coetzee, draw us into the passionate, associational flux of their own consciousness, which is full of bad, earnest, frankly essayistic ideas in noisy collision with each other and with life. In doing so they open the window of composition a little wider, pulling us into the foundational plane of writing itself, the noisy civil war an overactive sensibility imposes on itself, working through the cannon smoke of its own obsessions. Some readers find this clamor of competing ideas enervating, a distraction from the "real" drama of behavior and so on. For others like me it *is* the real drama, and it's the made-up characters with their appended costumes and behaviors that are the distraction.

And yet it's true that in the wrong hands, the articulation of ideas can be a drag on the fictive dream, narrowing its lift and spaciousness. If I ask a friend how he's doing and he says great, never better, you wouldn't believe it, and here's why—that is, if he's already articulated it for himself—then I generally regret having asked. On the other hand, if he hesitates or stammers or makes some random, belligerent, transparently defensive remark, ok, maybe I'll persevere. If he says rotten, dismal, hopeless, the pits, I'll cheerfully continue. But when he says nothing at all, when he groans and falls silent, leaving a chasm of awkward, sub-verbal tension that seems all but unbridgeable? Then I'm fully invested.

In the seam between rhetoric and reality there should be a friction, a complication, something that opens our perceptions instead of closing them off. "A writer," says Karl Kraus, "is one who makes a riddle out of an answer." Or as Grace Paley puts it in "A Conversation with My Father," a story that reads like a statement of *her* literary principles: "Everyone, real or invented, deserves the open destiny of life."

For an example of this friction take John Cheever's "Goodbye My Brother," a narrative that presents as a drama of sibling rivalry (there's a lot of sibling rivalry in Cheever) but in fact charts the collision of two partial and competing worldviews. The younger brother, Lawrence (or Tifty, as he's called), brandishes a relentless and depressingly rational X-ray vision against the thinly insulated indulgences of his family, while the narrator, his older sibling, struggles to uphold the aesthetic privileges of their old-WASP nostalgic codes—a world of soft light and soft music, where the country club dance is full of men dressed as football players and women as demure brides. The most interesting aspect of this rather neat schema is how often the narrator messes and subverts it, lapsing into inexplicable fits of dark, gloomy Tifty-vision himself:

> The fog blew around us like a cold smoke. I wished that it had been a clear night, because the easterly fog seemed to play into my misanthropic brother's hands. And I knew that the buoys . . . would sound to him like half-human, half-drowned cries, although every sailor knows the buoys are necessary and reliable fixtures, and I knew that foghorn at the lighthouse would mean wanderings and losses to him and that he could misconstrue the vivacity of the dance music . . . And I knew that Lawrence was looking at the party as he had at the weather-beaten shingles on our house, as if he saw here an abuse and a distortion of time; as if in wanting to be brides and football players we exposed the fact that, the lights of youth being put out in us, we had been unable to find other lights to go by and, destitute of faith and principle, had become foolish and sad.

You begin to feel that the story does not in fact require Tifty's presence at all, as his gloomy view of things has been seamlessly internalized to the point where it's the *narrator's* gloom that's the problem. Tifty himself is more like a symptom, a projection of some internal condition. His spirit, like the ghosts in "Turn of the Screw," roams the decaying house, a manifestation of the unwelcome truths his mother denies by drinking and his brother strives to evade or repress. If you don't believe me look at Cheever's own early drafts: there's no Tifty character to be found. The opposition of surly head and mushy heart is all embodied in the narrator. But Cheever, working through the story, chooses to literalize and externalize its dualities, making of them a sly philosophical comedy that is also about family dynamics and deep-worn grooves of conflict too. Here too, in the end, neither head nor heart—and we always err, it seems, on one side or the other—proves quite adequate. Who knows, maybe truth really *isn't* beauty; maybe they're forever separate and incompatible realities, absurdly joined, like the cat in another Cheever story, "The Country Husband," who runs around dressed in doll's clothes, his hairy tail swishing behind him. Or like Cheever himself, a randy aesthete trampling through the groomed gardens of Westchester County.

The commingling of oppositions yields tension and mystery, a grey area of anxiety between one alternative and another. In this messy room the writer sits. "Perhaps, being lost, one should get loster," Bellow writes in *Humboldt's Gift*. "Being very late for an appointment, it might be best to walk slower." The mystery of lostness is not uncertainty but a product of it, and possibly a solution: it makes good fiction slow down, travel sideways towards meaning like a crab, or burrow below it like a mole.

Speaking of moles let's pause to acknowledge the high priest of uncertainty, the prophet of paralysis: Franz Kafka. "Have you ever observed," he writes to Felice Bauer, his long-suffering fiancée, "how, within yourself and independent of other people, diverse possibilities open up in several directions, thereby actually creating a ban on your every movement?" In other words, don't wait up. The only relief for this condition, the only sphere of action available is the process of writing itself, where every plodding, painstaking new sentence is both a journey into future possibilities and the closing off of past ones. "When I am telling a story," he confesses, "I usually have the kind of feeling small children probably experience when attempting their first steps."

This is truly a kind of hunger art, nine parts frustration for every trace of inspiration. It proceeds from fantastical premises into quotidian, excruciatingly realistic situations—like the difficulties of getting out of bed or turning a doorknob when you're a bug, and the irritations that might subsequently arise from this transformation in one's nuclear family. The fantastical element in Kafka, as in Gogol, as later in Márquez, is as concentrated and contained as a drop of blood falling into water. But it changes property when it hits the water, becomes as formless and uncertain, as (in a sense) fantastically dull, as what we like to call normal life.

In the best stories, the prose gets in the act too, at once promoting and eroding certainties along the way—never content to do just one thing when it can, with what Babel calls "an almost invisible twist" do two ("The lever," he writes, "should rest in your hand, getting warm."). Take this passage from William Gass's "In the Heart of the Heart of the Country":

> Aunt Pet . . . has a water gaze, a smooth plump face despite her age, and jet black hair in a bun. She has the slowest smile of anyone I ever saw, but she hates dogs, and not very long ago cracked the back of one she cornered in her garden. To prove her vigor she will tell you this, her smile breaking gently while she raises the knob of her stick to the level of your eyes.

Our benignly and affectionately named Aunt Pet has slow watery features, which are both opposed and contained by the severe black bun atop her head. Her smile, gently, breaks. So does the dog's spine. So does our conventional idea of her as a sweet, conventional old lady. But it all happens slowly, unexpectedly, as if unconsciously—the same sneaky and deceptive way the knob of her stick rises into plain view.

Or this heartbreaking passage from Henry James:

> It came over him that never before—no, literally, never—had a lady dined with him at a public place before going to the play. The publicity of the place was just in the matter, for Strether, the rare, strange thing; it affected him almost as much as the achievement of privacy might have affected a man of a different experience. He had married, in the faraway years, so young as to have missed the natural time, in Boston, for taking girls to the Museum; and it was absolutely true of him—even after the close of the period of conscious detachment occupying the center of his life, the gray middle desert of the two deaths, that of his wife and that, ten years later, of his boy—he had never taken anyone anywhere.

The passage provides a kind of musical counterpoint to the experience of newness it alleges to discuss. For Strether, the wondrously novel action of going to dinner invokes his long gray history of *not* going to dinner, a point drummed home by the dolorous percussion of no's and never's that is his life, the things he has missed, the private intimacies he has failed to achieve, all the many anyones he has failed to take anywhere. This is the absolute truth of his life. And yet it arrives, as so often in James, after an arduous delay, obscured by fastidious qualifications and interruptions—we strain to locate it, and then strain some more to keep it in sight, through the fumbling twists and evasions—before revealing itself, starkly and to devastating effect, on the far side of the dashes.

The complexity of such a consciousness can't just be noted; it has to be *experienced*, manifested in the fabric and texture of the prose itself. Only words to play with: the writer's *cri de coeur*. The fact that words are not enough, are incapable of expressing the vagueness of our moods and longings, while discouraging, is also liberating, in that it makes it possible for writers to play with them in surprising ways, with ever evolving warps and woofs of suggestion. That we live in a relativistic universe full of wacky and competing signifiers may make it difficult to pin down a decisive meaning, but we go on trying anyway. We can't help it. The author isn't dead; he's just, like some Beckett character, footsore and tired. Nothing to say and no way to say it. Or wait: is it *no*thing, or *every*thing? Or is it both at once?

"What is required of us," Rilke writes in a letter, "Is that we love the difficult and learn to deal with it." He was talking about art, I think, but maybe he wasn't, maybe he was talking about life. In any case the difficult—or to use my word, the uncertainty—is all around us. We don't have to look very far to discover it. All we have to do is the hardest thing of all: to sit still at the desk as the world unmasks itself, rolling in ecstasy at our feet.

Emblem, Essence

When I was eighteen I tried to change my name for the second time. I had started out in life as a Robert, a nice dutiful name for a nice dutiful kid. Then at thirteen, as part of a general declaration of independence that included playing (badly) on the junior high football team, getting stoned (frequently) at bar mitzvahs, and exploring (all too rarely) the underside of girls' brassieres, I started calling myself Rob. Naturally I'd flirted with Bobby for a while, as one does, but Bobby seemed chirpy and diminutive; it lacked the gravitas I craved. The same with Bob, a name I did not care for at all. Frankly I did not much care for Rob either, but I preferred it to dull, palindromish Bob and to the bland, stilted formality of Robert. Rob had a certain velocity, a lean, suggestive note of thievery and transgression. This Rob fellow, whoever he was, may have been a nice Jewish boy, but he wasn't *only* a nice Jewish boy: he was also a dangerous character who stole trivial items from hard-working shopkeepers for no reason, as I did; performed unspeakable acts on himself in the privacy of his room, as I did; and skipped out of gym class when rope-climbing was required, as I did, to go smoke Kools in the parking lot with the other dangerous, rope-avoiding characters: the Daves (née Davids), the Matts (née Matthews), the Steves (née Stephens).

My parents of course continued to call me Robert. So did my brothers. So did my teachers. So did everyone else. This in some form or other went on for a long while.

At eighteen I went away to California and began what seemed to me a new, more interesting life. In recognition of this I decided to wipe the slate clean of the whole tedious Rob/Robert issue for good. I asked people to start calling me Butch—I mean, Jesse. Honestly I wasn't wild about Jesse either, but it was my middle name, and I'd run out of other options. I may have been a dangerous character but I wasn't so brazen as to go out and steal—that is, *rob*—a distant, utterly fraudulent name for myself. I had my integrity to consider, even if this integrity of mine was still largely theoretical.

"What is that [name], when all is said and done," Montaigne asks, "but a sound, or three or four strokes of a pen, so easy to vary in the first place? . . . What prevents my groom from calling himself Pompey the Great?"

Apparently nothing. So Jesse it was. Or rather wasn't. Because there was one small problem with my experiment in re-naming. It wasn't that virtually no one could remember to call me Jesse (though, in fact, virtually no one could remember to call me Jesse); it was that *I* couldn't remember to call me Jesse. On those rare occasions when someone did remember to call me Jesse they'd eventually wind up calling me Rob or Robert anyway, as well they should have, given that I consistently failed to answer to Jesse. To remember that I was now a Jesse and keep living my (let's face it) rather Rob-ish life at the same time took far too much energy; I could do one or the other, but not both. If renaming ourselves is an act of existential creation, a way of becoming—*pace* Ralph Ellison—our own fathers, then to become my own father while simultaneously remaining my own (still perfectly healthy) father's son was a trick I seemed unable to master. Maybe on some Oedipal level I didn't *want* to master it. Though God knows I tried.

But why am I going on about this, you're wondering?

For the past few years I've been working on a novel with two protagonists: one a small-town school principal yearning to bail out of his settled life, the other a feckless *luftmensch* from New York desperate to bail into one. The name of the New Yorker is Oren Pierce. I have known this about him from the start, before I knew what he looked like or what his problems were. The source of this knowledge is both mysterious and critical to me: I apprehend its power better when I don't have it. Meanwhile after three years I still don't know what to call my other main character, the school principal. As a place-holder I've been calling him Henry Gladfelter, but I have never liked this name and even he seems reluctant to answer to it. Meanwhile I have a file on my computer full of other potential names for him. There are sixty-five of these names, and counting. Lately a sense of Kierkegaardian despair has begun to set in, a sense that that no one name is of greater value and appeal than the collective potentiality of all the other, equally possible names, so I find it hard to call him anything—other than Henry Gladfelter, a name I don't like.

And by the way, neither does anyone else. In fact when I ran it by my editor (who will remain nameless, like God) he *hated* the name Henry Gladfelter, which struck him, he said, as heavy-handed, overdetermined, didactic; it showed, he said, "the touch of a gorilla." I found this interesting, as to my knowledge there had been no intention in the choice at all. I'd chosen the name at random, ripped it off from a building I'd given a lecture in once, a fairly undistinguished building at that. If anything, it was *under*determined. But my editor didn't care. He suggested I find a name that had no referential or allegorical resonance, a name that was interesting and musical and colorful—a name, he said, "distinctive rather than emblematic." Think of Nabokov, he said. Think of Bellow. What would *they* call him?

I was silent. I had no fucking clue what they'd call him. But it seemed clear I better get one. Because if I couldn't get this one lousy name right, what hope was there for the book itself?

"I have to have the name to start a novel," Elmore Leonard wrote. "If I don't have the right name, I can't write it." Clearly, with forty-plus novels to his credit, Leonard found a way. Meanwhile I keep fiddling with my lists like a casting director, raiding box scores and obituaries and the occasional metropolitan-area phone book for potential candidates. And so the grid-lock builds. If my former therapist was still around, he'd surely point out that this fiddling is a neurotic activity designed to hold off the more demanding activity of writing the novel, and doubtless he'd be right. My former therapist, by the way, is named Mark Snyder, not a good name for him at all.

Writers are reliant upon names as tourists are reliant upon landmarks, as religious people are reliant upon prayers: they help us crystallize our still-vague desires, lend form to the surrounding formlessness, project onto the bewildering existence of imagined things a sound and shape we can apprehend. At the same time we resent the very arbitrariness, the flimsy, random quality of our own naming constructions. Only God (not much of a name, really, just a bit of generic shorthand) do we hold exempt, letting him slide by with that glib, near-tautological moniker, "I am that I am." (I am talking about the Hebrew God, of course, not the Muslim God, for whom there are ninety-nine names, all of them quite flattering.) The rest of us must submit to being named like the other animals. And yet unlike the other animals we're at once conscious of alternatives and made restless by that consciousness. Like adolescent children, we resist any attempts to define us: we hate our bodies, our hair, our clothes; our names sit upon our personalities like ill-fitting crowns, the same way our heads, which don't fit either, sit upon our necks.

Perhaps this is why expectant parents understand the problem of naming—the necessity for it, and the maddening, paralyzing arbitrariness of it—all too well. It's instructive to browse through baby-naming books, checking out the hot names, the Malcolms and Emmas and Rosies and so on, and comparing them to the hot names of previous generations. There are entire blocks on the Upper West Side where every boy is a Sam or a

Max or a Jake, where the preschool class list is like a roll call of the *alter kockers* who once hung out scratching their balls at the neighborhood *shvitz*. My own generational cohort, on the other hand, tend to have the sort of dull postwar suburban names—Jay and Jim and John and so on—I would never inflict upon a fictional character in a million years. And yet when I actually picture these people in my head, they're far from dull.

Which raises a question: is a rage to lend color and energy to our children and fictional characters, to provide them with a jazzy, distinctive emblem that will follow them through life, merely a displaced form of narcissism? And does it matter? Once upon a time a kid called Robert Zimmerman changed his name: changed it all the way to Bob. True he reached for the lyric stars with that Dylan. But would he have caught them, would he have joined them, were it not for that drolly understated and enigmatic launch pad, that boring Bob?

The fact that "Call me Ishmael" is *not* the first phrase of *Moby Dick* comes as a surprise to a lot of us, as it's the line we remember best, and introduces so efficiently the epistemological challenges ahead. (It's never clear for example if Ishmael is actually *named* Ishmael; he may just want us to call him that.) And yet the book's actual first phrase—"Etymology"—is arguably even more fitting, warning us at the outset that, like the Usher who bids us enter the narrative's labyrinth, we have an awful lot of pale, dusty research to perform if we are going to understand how names attach to things. And even then we might never get there. The rage generated by too much pointless scholarship is, as any graduate student knows, considerable. An ontological quest that can't be fulfilled, a bottomless thirst that can't be slaked—these things test our sanity. So too with Ahab. For naming too is a kind of harpooning. When we want to define something we speak of "pinning things down." But the whiteness of the whale *can't* be pinned down, it can only be described, and apprehended, and more than a little feared, another emblem of nature's vast and terrible impersonality, which shrugs off the impositions of human will like so many toy harpoons. Ishmael survives the ordeal because he learns the crucial lesson: that the world remains separate from the names we append to it. Rather than strap himself to the whale's back, as Ahab does both literally and figuratively, he achieves a little distance, a space between. It isn't much. But in that space he can tell his tale.

Donald Barthelme's marvelous essay, "Not Knowing," also contends with the challenge of naming, the consequences of using language to represent a non-lingual essence. Of course Barthelme is as skeptical of language's claims to solidity as the next meta-fictionist. Nonetheless he strikes an intriguing compromise between relativist and absolute (or post- and premodern) modes, exhibiting a stubbornly atavistic, almost *Ahab- istic* faith in the Word:

> We do not mistake the words "the taste of chocolate" for the taste of chocolate itself, but neither do we miss the tease in "taste", the shock in "chocolate". Words have halos, patinas, overhands, echoes. . . . The combinatorial agility of words, the exponential generation of mean- ing once they're allowed to go to bed together, allows the writer to surprise himself, makes art possible, reveals how much of Being we haven't yet encountered.

An example of this patina effect, this distinct lingering residue of per- sonality, is the human voice: the way it plays on our nerve receptors and emotional muscle memory, the way, when someone calls us on the phone after many years, we recognize their voice right away. It's like that old joke about the woman who answers the phone, "Hello?" "Listen," a man says, "I know you, and I know everything that you want, and I'm going to come over there and throw you on the floor and do all those dirty things to you." "Wait," she says, "you know all this from hello?"

Names too, like voices, are charged with what Laurence Sterne in *Tristram Shandy* calls "magick bias." For some people (ok, me) the names of old ballplayers, possibly because we encountered them first on the radio, stimulate our nervous system like cookies in Proust. Joe Pepitone. Horace Clarke. Lindy McDaniel. Dooley Womack. Just calling the roll of that class of feckless bumblers, the 1967 Yankees (final record: 72–90) plunges me into a foamy memory-bath that smells suspiciously like Schlitz. Call it *the connoisseurship of the particular*. There's no objective value to recalling these names, they're of no use to me whatsoever, and yet here they still are, loitering in my head four decades later, taking up per- fectly good space. A reminder, we might say, of having lived. Faded stick- ers on memory's suitcase, at once interchangeable and, in some paradoxi- cal way, irreplaceable.

But context matters. Once, when I was living in Houston and knew no one, I went down to a pawn shop and bought a twelve-inch TV. The guy behind the counter examined my check skeptically, frowning through the bulletproof glass. "Cohen, eh? What kind of name is that? Don't see it much around here." I nearly kissed the man. I had just left a New York apartment building that featured seven different mailboxes with the name Cohen. The Columbia alumni magazine had just run an article, by a guy named Robert Cohen, about all the other Robert Cohens he had encountered in his research, in which someone he called "the novelist Robert Cohen" made an appearance, whom I am pretty sure was me. On the other hand, I could be wrong. I wasn't reading too closely. There's a certain disassociation that sets in when you see your own name in print. A sense that this can't be *me*. That a name, any name, is just some weird hieroglyph, some assemblage of black marks scratched on a page. A stick-figure, not a self.

This may account for the peculiar spell that's broken—or established—when one encounters the increasingly familiar device of a writer using their own name in a novel. To discover that the author has been pulled into the fabric of the work, reduced to a character among other characters, was once a profound, vaguely surreal surprise. "That novels should be made of words, and merely words, is shocking," William Gass wrote. "It's as though you had discovered that your wife were made of rubber." Of course like any device it grows less shocking as it's repeated, which it often is. But even now it retains a little naughty, undermining thrill. After all, if the writer's real name and circumstances can be enlisted into the work, where does it stop? Might we too risk being drafted, forced to don the uniform of a character in our own—or worse, someone else's—novel?

Still, to use "real" names in a fictional work is a tricky business, as real names carry with them a set of preexistent truths and correspondences the author feels duty-bound to acknowledge and treat with respect. Say we write about something that actually happened, but change the names to avoid hurt feelings or whatever. Do we risk a diminishment in intensity, in authority, in authenticity? Obviously no one cares if I change my Uncle Max's name, in the process of writing about him, to Uncle Sherman (and Sherman is probably better, come to think of it, less familiar, less clichéd than Max—Max!). Nor will my Uncle Max be offended, as he's long dead, and even when he was alive he was never much of a reader. Nonetheless to change his name would be a mistake, I feel, the sort of minor, inconsequential lie that spreads like a stain, tainting the fabric around it. Better to use the real, irreplaceable name of my Uncle Max, who was pretty real and irreplaceable himself, come to think of it, a rather brilliant but extremely passive and phlegmatic person who worked all his life for the postal service and sat on the sofa of his Co-op City apartment kvetching about the Yankees. He had a twin brother Jack who did change his name, by the way, to Callen, God alone knows why. Maybe Cohen didn't sound Jewish enough. On the other hand it wasn't like he was discarding some treasured family heirloom. The name Cohen went back only a few years; it had been imposed upon my paternal grandfather at Ellis Island, in lieu of the *real* "real" family name, Kelemeyitz—which coming as it did from a shtetl in Ukraine that had itself been named and renamed too many times to count, at the whim of whichever quasi-fascist power happened to be in vogue at the time, no one on earth could be bothered to spell.

Which is to say, even "real" names often turn out to be invented, fictitious. The current geneology craze is constantly turning up ancestors we didn't know we had, odd turns of fate's wheel that have endowed us with wayward nationalities, bone structures, and last names, none of whose origins can be traced back to a fixed or definitive source. Slave names are of course the most grotesque example. In light of which the namelessness of Ellison's Invisible Man proves instructive. By allowing himself that imaginative out, he bids to free himself from the labels history has and continues to impose upon him, to strip away all the false names and false selves in pursuit of some essential legacy or identity that lies below, waiting to be discovered. To be *claimed*. At the end of the novel it's still not clear if he has done so. But like Ishmael, he has carved out a small, illuminated space in which to write his story. To be, for a change, not the victim of events but the one who isolates and names them, who gives them shape.

A good name, like a good sentence, negates its own alternatives. The very sound of it, the noise it makes, immediately becomes inevitable, beyond question. Any name that isn't good in this sense is de facto *bad*, in that it tears a small gap in the fictive dream, one that reminds us not just of the writer's tin ear but the precariousness of all literary endeavors. This danger is not confined to naming alone, but to language itself, the *mot juste* and all that.

Of course the *mot un-juste*, the *mot merdre*, can be useful too, if it's bad enough, which is to say so ridiculously bad it's inspired. Think of Humbert Humbert, a name chosen by the protagonist himself, or so Nabokov would have us think. Think of Hardy's Bathsheba Everdene; of West's Balso Snell; Heller's Milo Minderbinder; of Flannery O'Connor's Manley Pointer and Hulga Hopewell and Hazel Motes; of Waugh's Tony Last and John Beaver; of Pynchon's Oedipa Maas and Stanley Koteks and Tyrone Slothrop . . . of all the silly, extravagantly over-determined comic-book names that wave their own ludicrousness in the air like a flag, alerting us to satiric fires in progress. Like the hooded, cigar-smoking Klansmen of Philip Guston (née Goldstein), their very cartoonishness is the point, a comically grotesque shorthand for a world gone to extremes. And yet there's something warmly endearing about them too. A shlumpy, betrodden humanity that just may survive the flames, albeit hooded, albeit reduced.

It's the other kind of bad names, the names that try too hard to be emblematic and distinctive—that show, in my editor's phrase, *the touch of the gorilla*—that writers tend to fret over in the dark, when they would much rather be sleeping. And those who don't fret probably should. Henry James for example, after a promising start (Daisy Miller, Isabel Archer) became, in his late-dictatorial years, notoriously awful at naming his characters. Lambert Strether? Hyacinth Robinson? Fleda Vetch? Morgan Mallow? Booby Manger? Merton Densher? It's as if they've been purchased at bulk discount from some seedy, fly-by-night retail establishment selling Dickens knock-offs. Dickens' own Book of Memoranda contained almost two hundred names, many of them lifted from death notices. He too was reluctant to write the novel without them. This may account for the gleeful air of hyper-functionality, of preloaded narrative meaning, that surrounds his Scrooges and Gradgrinds, his Pecksniffs and Murdstones and Bounderbys, landmarks on the vast, intricate map of the plot, staking out tonal planes and spatial geometries from which their respective novels can't be extricated. But Henry James is another story. What fit of loginess or perversity can we pin to the tail of Fanny Assingham? For the mandarin, fastidious Master to stamp his characters with the very vulgarity and crudeness he makes it his business, his Art, to elide and supersede, is an act of either supreme chutzpah or stratospheric cunning or baroque, egg-headed nuttiness, or possibly all of the above. And he's by no means the only offender out there on the canonical bookshelf. Hardy's Father Time: I mean, oy vey. And some of Graham Greene's heavy-handed names like (in *A Burnt Out Case*) Querry and Deo Gratias tilt the novel, in most ways a good one, towards the writer's worst tendencies: his symbolic neatness, the tight, airless schematicism he occasionally substitutes for that other tight and airless schema, orthodox faith.

Faulkner on the other hand claimed the only thing of genius he *knew* he'd ever done was to name those people Snopes. And Truman Capote's Holly Golightly (née Lulu Mae), in its brazen, glittering, self-willed artificiality (reminiscent of Capote's own mother Nina, née Lillie Mae) is yet another outsized American invention, along the lines of Fitzgerald's famous Mr. Gatz.

Like Joyce, Fitzgerald revels in the music of naming, the power generated by its sonic fission. Think of the way Daisy and Buchanan work together, the bright, trilling, floral femininity of the first locked away behind the massive power and reach, the run-on complacency of her marriage (that extra "an") to the second. And he doesn't stop there. On the merest pretext he invents a two-page list of visitors to Gatsby's house that summer, a rather whimsical litany of fantastical personages: *S. B. Whitebait, James B. Rotgut Ferret, George Duckweed, S. W. Belcher, Miss Claudia Hip*. This sense of relish and appetite shows up in Nabokov too—first in the notorious aria of ardor that opens the first chapter, that onomatopoetic lesson in how the tongue conspires with the teeth and the mouth (among other organs) to savor the taste of its own invention, that timeless, mythic, and much-molested name; and then in the poem-like list of Lolita's classmates in Ramsdale, including those celestial lesser angels Virginia McCoo, Vivian McCrystal, and Aubrey McFate, a poem Humbert has learned, he tells us, "by heart."

And then there's Bellow, whose restless exuberance is forever animating and distorting the names of his characters, and their physiognomies too. Valentine Gersbach, Victor Wulpy, Max Zetland, Von Humboldt Fleisher . . . such portraits, in their refusal to ever be pedestrian or dull, occasionally have the paradoxical effect of wearing us down a little, stranding us in a sea of bright, highly peculiar creatures who never shut up. To be fair, all this colorful crowd-noise is a feature of the work, not a bug. When *Seize the Day*'s Tommy Wilhelm (not his real name) enters a crowded subway tunnel, he sees "in every face the refinement of one particular motive or essence—*I labor, I spend, I strive, I design, I love, I cling, I uphold, I give way, I envy, I long, I scorn, I die, I hide, I want*." To give each soul an essence, and each body a name and a face that captures that essence, and then to set those essences in clamorous collision with each other, and with the weight of money, eros, and power and a whole lot of wild, half-articulated ideas—this is Bellow's operating system. He's no psychological realist, dealing with the small betrayals and moral crises of your basic Jims and Bills and Bobs; he's a brilliant caricaturist, and unusually for a caricaturist, a rather generous one. He bestows his characters with distinctive names the same way he bestows them with distinctive faces and bodies: with a bounce and a flourish, with something like love. ("*Love*," he writes in *Humboldt's Gift*, "*is gratitude for being*."). His names are emblematic expressions of an inescapable essence. It's no accident that Wilhelm's bid for Oedipal independence involves changing his name to Tommy—an experiment, like my own with Jesse, transparently doomed to fail. In his own mind, as in that of his stubbornly implacable father, he will forever remain a "Wilky."

The recognition that character is fate, and the refusal to make peace with that, illuminates the long, disastrous path of name-changing in literature. Flannery O'Connor's Joy Hopewell, in "Good Country People," renames herself Hulga as an act of ontological spite towards her twinned creators, her mother and God, denying herself the joy and innocence that is her true birthright. That her denial is revealed, in a twist as outrageous and bleakly funny as any story ever written, as yet another *expression* of that innocence, is an irony almost too much for her or the reader to bear. A similar tragic arc is traversed in a good deal of American fiction, with its insistence on self-invention, self-renewal. It's the story of Bernard Malamud's Henry Freeman (née Levin) in "Lady of the Lake," who in an effort to deny his own Jewish-particularist past loses the love of a woman who turns out to be a Holocaust survivor. And of the former Bruce J. Fein in Leonard Michaels' "Finn":

> *"Millicent," he whispered, shoving against her hand.*
> *"Fein," she whispered.*
> *"Finn," he said.*
> *She pulled free. "I think I need a cigarette. I mean I really need a cigarette, but I'd like to talk a little."*
> *Minutes later Finn was tapping the steering wheel with his fingernails. "I'm the only one who knows you're Jewish?"*
> *"Well, actually, my mother converted years and years ago."*

So goes the bitter comedy of assimilation: there's no getting free. You cast your name upon the waters and it comes floating back. Every effort to yank out your roots leaves you that much more ensnared. It's like something out of Sisyphus, or Camus, like something out of Borges or Kafka.

Kafka's own method of naming was, like all other aspects of his work, so bound up in his personal sense of deprivation as to approach the fantastical, though his descriptions of it tend to be numbingly rational and pragmatic. "Georg," he says of the hero of "The Judgment," "has the same number of letters as Franz. In Bendemann, the 'mann' is there only to strengthen the syllable 'Bende' . . . but Bende has the same number of letters as Kafka, and the vowel 'e' is repeated in the same position as the vowel 'a' in Kafka," etc. Perhaps this explains why the later we get in Kafka's oeuvre the leaner and more provisional the names become, until at last they are only stick-figure initials, barely able to prop themselves up.

By the time we come to Beckett, we have entered a realm of terminal skepticism regarding the applicability of any name at all. In Beckett's trilogy we enter a world not of composition and accrued meaning but of *de*composition, a language that yearns towards its own obliteration, a world comprised, as the *Unnameable*'s unnamed narrator says, of three essential conditions: the inability to speak, the inability to remain silent, and solitude. "There is no name for me, no pronoun for me, all the trouble comes from that." Molloy's mother insists on calling him "Dan." "I don't know why," he says, "my name is not Dan. Dan was my father's name perhaps, yes, perhaps she took me for my father. I took her for my mother and she took me for my father." As an act of revenge, or homage, or maybe just total confusion, he calls her "Mag, when I had to call her something":

> And I called her Mag because for me, without my knowing why, the letter g abolished the syllable Ma, and as it were spat on it, better than any other letter would have done. And at the same time I satisfied a deep and doubtless unacknowledged need, the need to have a Ma, that is a mother, and to proclaim it, audibly. For before you say mag you say ma, inevitably. . . . I had been living so far from words so long, you understand . . . even my sense of identity was wrapped in a namelessness often hard to penetrate, as we have just seen I think. . . . Yes, even then, when already all was fading, waves and particles, there could be no things but nameless things, no names but thingless names. I saw that now, but after all what do I know now about then, now when the icy words hailed down upon me, the icy meanings, and the world dies too, foully named.

In the work of Don DeLillo we find a similar, Beckett-like trajectory from noisy jabber towards ever-receding silence, an underground vocabulary of buried or secret names. "A secret name is a way of escaping the world," says a character in—what else?—*The Names*. The alternative to the mass language of global corporate esperanto (Mita, Suntory) is a sort of cargo cult of withholding and deferral and effacement. "The withheld work of art is the only eloquence that's left." So says that consummate cult writer, Bill Gray of *Mao II*. Bill Gray. Except Bill Gray is not his real name. His "real" name, if a fictional character in a fictional narrative can be said to have one, is Willard Skansey: the name of "a welterweight fighting outdoors in steaming holiday weather before a crowd of straw hats."

Amidst these showy, high-concept strategies the cool clarity of a novel like Marilynne Robinson's *Housekeeping* can start to seem the most radical departure of all. "My name is Ruth," the narrator begins, quietly but firmly, with a simple declarative echo of her biblical namesake. Ruth's sister, from whom she will become estranged existentially but not spiritually, is named Lucille, and we can hear in those two names (one shorn, stark, uncompromising; the other pretty, bright, outward-moving) and in the ethereal, uncontainable sound of their aunt's first name (Sylvie) combined with the half-benevolent menace of her last (Fisher), everything we need to know about the tragedy that follows. Of Robinson's names we can say they fulfill all our hopes and expectations and then some. They're at once subtly distinctive and subtly emblematic; they refuse to unpack their own secrets, but they manifest those secrets, in the form of stubborn, incontrovertible essences, on every page.

The incantation of names casts a spell, a heady mixture of magic and bias. Whitman speaks of repeating his own name over and over, and never growing tired of it, while Kipling notes a tendency among the "Asiatics" to throw themselves into "a mazement by repeating their own names over and over again to themselves, letting the mind go free upon speculation as to what is called personal identity . . . in a minute—in another half second—he felt he would arrive at the solution of the tremendous puzzle." Whisper the right word, and the door of personality swings open. But what is the right word?

There's a concept in translation called the *hapax legomenon*—a word or phrase in a text which, because it only occurs once, is notoriously difficult to interpret. Like nonce words, the *hapax legomenon* has either been coined for a single usage or has accidentally wound up that way, and thus fulfills our best hopes for all named things: a moniker that lives on forever, mysteriously, irreducibly; that becomes, in the end, its own text and context, its own emblem and essence both. I would like to call this the highest form of naming but of course I can call it whatever I like, as I can call myself whatever I like, and what difference does it make? Still, the best names I've ever personally come up with embody no fixed principle at all, leaving no clear paths that can be traced back to the dark woods of their own conception. They Are That They Are, basically. The same might even be true of Robert Cohen, G-d help him. Because who would ever make up a name like that?

The Piano Has Been Drinking

On the Art of the Rant

⌒⦇⦈⌒

It could and probably should be argued that the last thing we need in this country is another rant. God knows our cultural discourse is not what you'd call demure. If you're fully tuned in, if you listen to the radio and watch cable TV and waste a lot of time on social media, as I do, then your head is swimming with rants already, the dome of your consciousness divided like a multiplex into talking, or rather shouting, heads. In truth, if one wishes to be heard in this maelstrom, the really smart thing to do, as well as the most artful, is to chill: cool things down, be mild and judicious, perhaps even whisper.

Not that anyone would listen. How could they? Try typing "Rants" into Google and you will promptly gain access to some 1,700,000 very noisy and intemperate entries along the lines of this:

> *Here I start to speak on things that piss me off, and there are a lot of them. So shut up and read or leave.*
> *Topics:*
>
> *WHY I HATE HIPPIES*
> *I AM ALWAYS RIGHT*
> *WHY SMALL COLLEGES BLOW*
> *THINGS ASSHOLES SAY*
> *WOE IS ME*
> *THINGS ASSHOLES SAY II*
> *GET SOME MANNERS ASSHOLE*
> *EAT ME*

Indeed, with so many people ranting into the void, it's tempting to say writers should go the other way, tap those powers of command generated by judicious restraint. But restraint, like any muscle, can tighten up from overuse. Eventually it gets brittle and stiff, flexing compulsively in a way that's not judicious or restrained at all. Restraint in short is only powerful if it's restraining *something*, some vast, hot, brilliant, all-but-unrestrainable force of nature which we fear to gaze on too directly, lest we go blind. You can't have one without the other. Or can you?

Take that old commonsensical chestnut, "All things in moderation." As a rule of thumb this holds up nicely—unless one happens to be sitting in a really good restaurant, say, on someone else's expense tab, or driving a brand new sports car down a vacant coastal highway, or witnessing some small, pointlessly brutal act of cruelty or injustice being perpetrated on a helpless stranger. At such times no, I'm sorry, but moderation in all things isn't moderate at all. It's radical and extreme and unnatural, altogether wrong. It's more fitting to apply the idea of moderation in all things, as Oscar Wilde once quipped, to moderation itself. Because the best life— and art—does not so much disdain excess as embrace it, channel it, try to investigate it, and arguably in the process even moderate it a little too. If the heightened perception art both draws from and inspires depends upon the very extremes of mood, impulse, and yearning we spend the bulk of our lives repressing, then the writer's task is to explore that tension, to attune his or her instrument to that intrepid, unruly, often quite undomesticated inner music. To wander off towards the far borders of what's thinkable, what's sayable, and what's doable; testing the fence posts for sway; refusing to make nice, go home, sit tight, shut up.

"But you complain so all the time," says the young wife to her husband in Paul Bowles' *The Sheltering Sky.*

"Oh, not about life;" he replies, "only about human beings."

Does one celebrate human life, or sully it, by railing against its conditions and constrictions? "Perhaps man, like a blacksmith, seeks live coals, the hammering of iron on iron," writes Neruda, whose *Canto General* can be read as one long, variegated rant born of betrayal and exile. "That severity may be a condition of happiness."

The bilious discontent of the ranter is an ontological cry of the heart, a pounding for entry upon the stony, intractable gates of knowledge. Like all cries of the heart it begins as one small, focused complaint and then expands, falling in love with its own intensity, expanding its range of targets, shamelessly repeating itself, performing a kind of scorched-earth passion play that becomes over time less an urgent form of communication than an annoying, even boring distraction. Which is why we sane, sober types may shy away. Cross the street, over to the sunnier side, and get on with our business. After all, we don't *want* to scorch the earth. It's all we can do just to go on *living* on this damn planet, which is plenty scorched enough already, thank you. Why antagonize it further?

No, for most of us, our tendency when confronted by the hot lava of excessive emotion, in art as in life, is to arch an eyebrow, Letterman-style, and affect an air of bemused, ironic condescension, as if the asbestos of sheer knowingness might dampen all flames. It seems as good a strategy as any, which is to say it's the easiest, most reflexive one, the one we've already mastered without quite being conscious of having done so. Never mind that our knowingness is defensive, our ironic cleverness and moral relativism a shallow bluff; it will do. And if the price we pay is a bland, temperate art, with spoils so meager they hardly seem battling over or for; if we're no longer inclined to pick fights with each other over aesthetic matters, or even manage to convince ourselves such matters are *worth* fighting over, so be it. At least we'll all get along.

Nonetheless it can still be instructive, if not inspiring, to encounter artists who either can't or won't resist picking fights with each other, and with us, and sometimes with God, but nearly always with themselves— themselves most of all.

It can and has been argued that power and meaning in fiction are generated less by language than by music, a flow of sounds that become language almost by default. Think of Nabokov's lecture on Gogol's "The Overcoat"—

> The story goes this way: mumble, mumble, lyrical wave, mumble, fantastic climax, mumble, mumble, and back into the chaos from which they all derived. At this superhigh level of art, literature appeals to that secret depth of the human soul where the shadows of other worlds pass like the shadows of nameless and soundless ships.

Or that great Tom Waits song, "The Piano Has Been Drinking"—a gorgeous, sodden sailor's dirge of complaint, characterized by spiraling repetitions and a slow, slurry, maddeningly circular beat.

> The piano has been drinking, my necktie is asleep
> And the combo went back to New York, the jukebox has to take a leak
> And the carpet needs a haircut, and the spotlight looks like a prison
>   break
> And the telephone's out of cigarettes, and the balcony is on the make
> And the piano has been drinking, the piano has been drinking . . .
>
> And the menus are all freezing, and the light man's blind in one eye
> And he can't see out of the other

And the piano-tuner's got a hearing aid, and he showed up with his
    mother
And the piano has been drinking, the piano has been drinking
As the bouncer is a sumo wrestler cream-puff casper milktoast
And the owner is a mental midget with the IQ of a fence post
'cause the piano has been drinking, the piano has been drinking . . .

And you can't find your waitress with a Geiger counter
And she hates you and your friends and you just can't get served
    without her
And the box-office is drooling, and the bar stools are on fire
And the newspapers were fooling, and the ash-trays have retired
'cause the piano has been drinking, the piano has been drinking
The piano has been drinking, not me, not me, not me, not me, not me

Here we find the Ranter's full, albeit impotent arsenal—the long, fastidiously detailed catalogue of his failures; the drunken energies of his obsessions; the giddy flights of his projections; the agitated, overstated, maddeningly proliferating too-muchness of *every fucking thing*—all steaming furiously inside him, pushing him up and over the edge of what one can reasonably and temperately bear. Down the foamy flume he plunges, protesting his innocence all the way, deep into the reservoir of his most self-annihilating shames, at the bottom of which lies a black, impersonal hole that may swallow him completely. Whether this would be a catastrophe or a relief isn't clear. Perhaps touching bottom is the first, necessary step towards ascent. "A sting touches and arouses us better than something pleasant," writes Montaigne. And so with the Waits song. The narrator's pain arouses his powers of perception and attention, elevating everything in his purview, from the sleeping necktie to the deaf piano tuner to the aggressively hateful waitress to the blazing bar stools, to a feverish metaphoric pitch, the hot fire of his alienation spreading unchecked, feeding on itself as fires do.

"There is no love of life," Camus tells us, "without despair of life." And, we'd like to think, vice versa.

The Ranter, in short, like his fellow-sufferers at the bar, the Cynic and the Depressive, is a disappointed life-lover, another in a series of failed Romantics—an all too common (and generally White male) figure both on and off the page. Unlike his more introverted pals however, the Ranter hasn't learned, or refuses to learn, to suppress his disappointments. He can't help it. He has too many disappointments to deal with: there's no more room at the inn. He's full up, saturated, practically allergic; the slightest brush from disappointment's nettles gives him a rash, irritating old wounds, bringing his whole long history of disappointments to the surface, welling up and bleeding right through the skin. Irritation, like adolescence, is a sullen, restless, promiscuous condition: it likes to go out at night with other irritations, which it irritates and is irritated by in equal measure.

When all that inner restlessness and rage is projected outward, spattered like so much action painting onto the canvas of an indifferent world, we may find the world gloriously heightened and transfigured and illuminated in the process. Think of Milton's Satan. Of artists like Van Gogh, Francis Bacon, Lenny Bruce, H. L. Mencken, Thomas Bernhard. For that matter think of D. H. Lawrence, whose authorial stand-in *Kangaroo*, like *all* his authorial stand-ins (and the sitting author himself), "wearied himself to death struggling with the problem of himself and calling it Australia."

Lawrence of course is unavoidable in any discussion of Ranting, so let's get him out of the way, or embrace him I mean, straight off. Here's a paragraph from page 2 of his rather wacko late novella "St Mawr," in which the narrator describes one of the principle characters, a young fop named Rico:

> Rico was handsome, elegant, but mostly he had spots of paint on his trousers and he ruined a necktie pulling it off. He behaved in a most floridly elegant fashion, fascinating to the Italians. But at the same time he was canny and shrewd and sensible as any young poser could be, and, on principle, good-hearted, anxious. He was anxious for his future, and anxious for his place in the world, he was poor, and suddenly wasteful in spite of all his tension of economy, and suddenly spiteful in spite of all his ingratiating efforts, and suddenly ungrateful in spite of all his burden of gratitude, and suddenly rude in spite of all his good manners, and suddenly detestable in spite of all his suave, courtier-like amiability.

Note that the tug-of-war being fought over Rico's character in the narrator's (that is Lawrence's) sensibility—the moral relativism and sympathy which allows us to see him as at once transparently phony and also vulnerable and good-hearted—begins to wobble and tilt as the paragraph goes on, while that ranting impulse in Lawrence, that stewing spite, never far from the surface, heats like a microwave, fed by the electric current of his scrutiny. Pretty soon it steams up the windows entirely, obscuring the last traces of Forsterian judiciousness (you can see in the letters he wrote to Forster a near-compulsion to get a rise out of the man, to find some latent mean streak), until any serious narrative interest in Rico collapses, by paragraph's end, in a disgusted heap.

That this contemptible character Rico does not in fact *exist*, but is only a hasty, patched-together construct, a paper tiger, or target, for the author to shoot at, is worth noting here, if only as a reminder that every ferocious moralist requires some hateful object. If life neglects to supply enough of them, or even if it does, he'll go ahead and invent a few anyway. This is what ultimately gets so tiresome in Lawrence: this eternal shadow-boxing with phantoms of his own devising. After *Sons and Lovers*, the novels for all their frequent brilliance become increasingly afflicted with this compulsion, and suffer for it. The novel is after all a supremely inclusive and forgiving (read: *incredibly indulgent*) form, which means that formally speaking, there's nothing to shut Lawrence up. Perhaps this is why he's often at his best in his short stories, where the compressions of form hold the messy, garrulous expansiveness of sensibility beautifully and productively in check. Some genies *need* their bottles.

In Lawrence's short fiction, the emotional and literal violence feels dramatized and localized rather than asserted and imposed. I'm thinking of that amazing story "Tickets Please," with its wild, vengeful ending, where all the spurned women taken out by the rakish young conductor on what the narrator warns us is "the most dangerous tram service in England" converge upon him like animals, tear his clothes off his back and practically strangle him before hurrying off at the end "with mute, stupefied faces." It's as if the violence is both cause and symptom of the white space around it, this transitional interlude with the men off at war, the women—briefly—in power, and the future up in the air. And yet there's no time to linger. Soon the bus will arrive at its stop, and the writer and his women will go home, recompose themselves, tamp down their murderous, atavistic instincts, and overcook the usual vegetables for dinner.

When the clock is turned off, however, when the fences are down and the requirements of form no longer obtain, we get the Other Lawrence— the soapbox-straddling, spittle-flying, late-Nietzchean who enjoys nothing so much as a good long rant. ("The older I get," he admits, or boasts, "the angrier I become, generally.") In this mode he recalls someone I used to encounter during my college years at Berkeley, affectionately known to us as the Hate Man. He was a scrawny bearded fellow who wore long dresses and splashed around the fountain in Sproul Plaza, yelling at everyone who wandered past, his syntax and vocabulary so similar to Lawrence's that it makes me wonder if the Hate Man was yet another rancorous and embittered refugee from Wheeler Hall, where the English Literature Department was located:

> No, I don't understand a bit what you mean about rightness and about relationships and about the world. Damn the world anyhow. And I hate "understanding" people, and I hate more still to be understood. Damn understanding more than anything. I refuse to understand you. Therefore you can say what you like, without a qualm, and never bother to alter it. I shan't understand.

Later in the same letter (to Earl Brewster) Lawrence's patience even for the language of impatience runs out altogether. No words can give sufficient shape and dimension to his all-encompassing rage. Instead he gives vent to a spasm of silly, sputtering onomatopoeia that recalls the old Batman show of the '60s ("Pfui!—pish, pshaw, prrr!") and is actually quite charming and funny if you have a sense of humor, which Lawrence of course didn't. Too bad. Because there's real gold to be mined from a guy who claims to hate "people who rave with unreasonable antipathies," or denounces a friend as "one of those irritating people who have generalized detestations." But comedy was not his thing.

However, all fun aside, it's always a mistake to condescend to Lawrence, or to dismiss his intemperant rages as the product of a surly temperament, even if they are. Because there's a genuine philosophy at work too. It may not be consistent, it may not make sense, it may not hold up to scrutiny, but there's something admirable in the man's aggression, his need for conflict, his tireless revolt against the passive drift of convention and a weightlessly secular culture—of, it often seems, *all* culture. "I am essentially a fighter," he admits. "To wish me peace is bad luck—except the fighter's peace . . . All truth—and real living is the only truth—has in it the elements of battle and repudiation." As he writes to a friend studying Buddhism:

> But always remember I prefer my strife, infinitely, to other people's peace, haven, and heavens . . . more and more I feel that meditation and the inner life are not my aim, but some sort of action and strenuousness and pain and frustration and struggling through . . . oh god, must one go the extreme limit, then to come back?"

Note that this is posed not as an answer but as a searching, rather beautiful question. It might serve as the epigraph to many spikey and ambitious works of literature, from Rimbaud to Conrad to Genet to Beckett, to contemporaries like Houellebeq and Carrère. That these names are not American is perhaps no accident. For American writers of recent generations, conditioned as we've been by irony and by the general insulations of middle-class life, reading Lawrence feels like a tiresome affront—so uncool, so repetitive, so over the top. He seems ill-suited to our age. It may be better to locate him, as Geoff Dyer does in his marvelous book on Lawrence, in the European tradition of Svevo and Walser and Thomas Bernhard, the literature of neurasthenia, of anxiety, fretting, and complaint, of what Lawrence calls "the life-exhaustion feeling." A feeling, as Dyer points out, weirdly akin to the *life-affirming* quality for which Lawrence, back in the sixties, was so admired.

Life exhaustion, life affirmation: these are nervous twins, not quite identical but forever linked ("there is no love of life without despair of life"). Anyone with any sense knows that to run around the world demanding an affirmation of your existence is a recipe for heartbreak. Fortunately for the rest of us, "sense" is not one of the ranter's virtues. They're emissaries of anti-sense, anti-reason. They're intruders who come crashing through the walls of our glass houses, yelling "FIRE!", alerting us to the hideous, fundamentally irrational quotient of suffering going on outside.

"In his terror of chaos," Lawrence writes in "Chaos in Poetry,"

> man fixes some wonderful erection of his own between himself and
> the wild chaos, and gradually goes bleached and stifled under his
> parasol. Then comes a poet, enemy of convention, and makes a slit
> in the umbrella; and lo! The glimpse of chaos is a vision, a window
> to the sun.

This is not so different in spirit from Chekhov's famous passage in "Gooseberries" about the man who in a better world would stand outside our houses, pounding upon the locked door of our complacencies.

> There ought to be behind the door of every happy, contented man
> someone standing with a hammer continually reminding him with
> a tap that there are unhappy people; that however happy he may be,
> life will show him her laws sooner or later, trouble will come for
> him—disease, poverty, losses, and no one will see or hear, just as
> now he neither sees nor hears others.

Thomas Bernhard, whether in homage or mockery (or both), puts his own hilariously negative black-on-black spin on this in his novel *Concrete*:

> There ought to be only happy people—all the necessary conditions are present—but there are only unhappy people.... The question is really only how we are to survive the winter as painlessly as possible. And the much crueler spring. And summer we've always hated. Then autumn takes everything away from us again. *Then she displayed the most ravishing bosom the world had ever seen.* I don't know why this sentence occurred to me just now and made me laugh. It doesn't matter either: what matters is that the laughter was entirely unforeseen.... We go through periods of agitation which can sometimes last for weeks and can't be switched off. Then suddenly they're gone.

That italicized eruption of lust in the middle is a wonderful reminder of the Ranter's gift for veering off the road—for sudden lapses and flights of lyrical intensity or savage humor. Once you have it, a license to cut loose gives permission for just about anything—the irrational, the non sequitur, the digressive, you name it. "Though the digression is not identical to the Rant," Charles Baxter says, "they are both children of that difficult but lovable father, Mr. Not-Getting-to-the-Point." The lineage of rambling, near-plotless volubility dates back at least to Lawrence Sterne, though it takes on darker hues as it approaches the present, becomes more of a complaint about the discontents of self. At least in the Northern hemisphere. In the South, we get books like Machado de Assis' *Epitaph of a Small Winner*—a pretty sunny affair for a book dictated by a corpse—and Humberto Costantini's *The Long Night of Francisco Sanctis*, and Roberto Bolaño's *By Night in Chile*, works that sucker-punch us, at the end, with the underlying political terror all that surface chattiness has been working so hard to hold back. To paper over.

Bernhard's narrators, on the other hand, remain largely in their own rooms, knocking into the furniture, rummaging through the overstuffed drawers of consciousness, snatching at whatever makes them maddest. There's a Chekhovian hammer at work, though it's not clear to what end. Then too any steady diet of hammering, if it isn't modulated, can grow as soporific as a steady diet of not-hammering. Even the urgent *whoop-whoop* of an emergency vehicle begins to take on, after a while, a glazed, trancey sound. So too with any extremes of tonality and voice: once we can predict their rhythms and parameters, their register and range, our attention can't help but fall off a little. Bernhard is well aware of this problem, of course. Nonetheless he can't help it, he's determined to test both us and himself. His prose unfurls as one long, unbroken, formidably dense paragraph; what makes it work is its sneakiness, its stubbornness, its relentlessness. The one-note quality turns out to be an entire monochromatic scale. It's like a Philip Glass opera, a dazzling spectacle that leaves us gaping, at once stupefied and awed.

The singular intensity of the Rant embodies savagery and humor, a pair of colliding extremes that often, as in Beckett, assume a slapstick or vaudeville form. The humor at once feeds off and undermines the anger. This strikes me, by the way, as a perfectly reasonable response to existence. True, one part of us is mad. One part of us prefers, as Rebecca West puts it, "the disagreeable to the agreeable, loves pain and its darker night despair, and wants to die in a catastrophe that will set life back to its beginnings and leave nothing of our house save its blackened foundations." But another part of us is *not* mad. Another part of us is drearily sane, a genuine straight man. And this part too must be accounted for, if the writing is not to degenerate into mere crankiness.

In Lawrence and Bernhard, in Beckett and Dostoevsky, this wrestling match between sense and sensibility becomes palpable, furious, sometimes exhausting. The Underground Man rails against an existence in which, to his infinite annoyance, two times two equals four. For him, reason—rational consciousness—is a closed, airless room. Dostoevsky's heroes, like Lawrence's and Bellow's and Malcolm Lowry's and countless others, turn their back on reason and "choose hell." Their suffering and failures are recast, by narrative alchemy, into the heroism of an indignant and tormented heart.

In Gilbert Sorrentino's poignant and audacious story, "The Moon In Its Flight," a working class Italian guy from Brooklyn falls in love with a middle class Jewish girl from the Bronx. Then of course he loses her. Then of course he writes a story about it, many years later, a bitter, lyrical, self-lacerating story, so feverish and intense as to almost, by sheer aesthetic willfulness, resuscitate the crushed hopes of his younger self, and redeem them too. True, this is more or less the story of every male writer who ever walked the earth. But that's more a feature of the narrative than a bug. The cartoonish familiarity of the subject matter is yet another defeat for our hero, yet another of life's (and art's) little traps he's powerless to escape. Like the Poe-obsessed Nabokov (whose inspiration for *Lolita*, he informs us, was the first drawing done by an ape in captivity: "this sketch showed the bars of the poor creature's cage") we can feel the jittery percussion of his bruised, tell-tale heart beating up through the story's floor, trying to free itself from the constrictions of time, space, memory, art, and dumb luck:

> Let me come and sleep with you. Let me lie in your bed and look at you in your beautiful pajamas. I'll do anything you say. I'll honor the beautiful father and mother. I'll hide in the closet and be no trouble. I'll work as a stock boy in your father's beautiful sweater factory. It's not my fault I'm not Marvin or Shelley. I don't even know where CCNY is! Who is Conrad Aiken? What is Bronx Science? Who is Berlioz? What is a Stravinsky? How do you play Maj-Jongg? What is schmooz, schlepp, Purim, Moo Goo Gai Pan? Help me . . .

This being, as the narrator reminds us, an American story, there's also some class warfare in the mix, along with a fusillade of erotic and aesthetic longings. The effect is like a raised fist, or finger, to the whole idea of emotion recollected in tranquility. Or is it? For all the heat of its arias and love songs, the story is (also) cunningly mediated by its shadow voice: that older, more prosaic, more embittered self who picks up the pieces of the dream ("turn *that* into a joke," he dares us) and tries hopelessly to fit them together on memory's coffee table. But the design eludes him. He's powerless to grasp the key that will unlock the self from its cell. All he can do, the poor creature, is bang his head against the bars of the cage. A reminder that the futility of literary endeavor is both fueled by and inextricable from the futility of life. It's all the same cage. "Art," the narrator bitterly concludes, "can't rescue anyone from anything."

Whether we should believe him is another story. Behind all the veils and personae there's another presence—I speak now of the reader—who is not just reading about an experience but *having* one. And a very gorgeous, bruising one at that. Which is to say that this story about the failure of stories, about the miserable inadequacy of stories, about all the flimsy, lurid contrivances to which miserable, inadequate stories resort in an effort to console us for our defeats, is itself a heady and exhilarating triumph. Turn *that* into a joke.

We might even say that turning things that can't be turned into jokes into jokes is its own form—the highest form—of art. It often seems that way, reading a writer like Beckett. Take any random passage from *Molloy*:

How difficult it is to speak of the moon and not lose one's head, the witless moon. It must be her arse she shows us always. Yes, I once took an interest in astronomy, I don't deny it. Then it was geology that killed a few years for me. The next pain in the balls was anthropology and the other disciplines, such as psychiatry, that are connected with it, disconnected, then connected again, according to the latest discoveries. What I liked in anthropology was its inexhaustible faculty of negation, its relentless definition of man, as though he were no better than God, in terms of what he is not.

Et cetera. What's being decried as well as celebrated here is less a social injustice than an existential one: the fact that we humans are only what we are, if that. We're not generally comfortable with this sort of fatalism. We like to think of people, or ourselves anyway, as perfectible, capable of genuine goodness and niceness, at least on those occasions where we aren't being sociopathic, racist, or violent. Because niceness is our default mode, we don't care to be harangued on the subway and told we're living the wrong life altogether. We prefer to feel like it's morning here, not evening. We prefer figures who are positive-minded and embrace multitudes. That's why we like Whitman, and leave Poe to the French. That's why we prefer early Twain to late Twain, and certain passages in Melville to other passages in Melville. We'd much rather head off to sea in a spirit of giddy exhilaration than be trapped in an office with Bartleby, staring joylessly into an airshaft. And yet, here we are. Why? Is it simply a question of human nature? Was the Puritan tradition, with its hellfire moralism, its boom-and-bust cycles of indulgence and repentance, always destined to lead us here?

Maybe we should blame those European imports, the Jews, who are famously quick to complain about stuff. Those black bags brought over in steerage were heavy with grievances, the language a litany of kvetches, their sacred texts a thicket of quarrels and lamentations, going all the way back to Job.

Everyone is familiar with the iconic figure of Sholom Aleichem's Tevya the Dairy Man, his village crumbling, his family falling away from him, his horse, or mule, inadequate to the task, who raises his fist to the heavens and argues with his Maker in an angry, bewildered, and tremendously catchy way. But some songs are more like a dirge. In Stanley Elkin's "Criers and Kibitzers, Kibitzers and Criers" we find Greenspahn, who has recently lost his son, whirling angrily down the drain of his life, succumbing to rage, grief, and entropy even as his grocery story succumbs to the inevitable pull of the chains. He is, we might say, bound up in these chains, and what's worse is he no longer cares. Or rather, he does and he doesn't. Whatever line once existed between caring and not-caring, between living and dying, between cataloguing in masochistic detail the trivial little objects that wall him in (Job was very good at this too) and seeing through them to nothing, has gone blurry, and his own failure to recognize the reason—the unshed tears that cloud his perception, the unchanneled grief that takes the form of rage and stasis—is his tragic condition, in which he will be spared no indignities:

> In the afternoon Greenspahn thought he might be able to move his bowels. He went into the toilet off the small room at the back of the store. He sat, looking up at the high ceiling. In the smoky darkness above his head he could just make out the small, square tin ceiling plates. They seemed pitted, soiled, like patches of war-ruined armor. Agh, he thought, the place is a pigpen. The sink bowl was stained dark, the enamel chipped, long fissures radiating like lines on the map of some wasted country. The single faucet dripped steadily. Greenspahn thought sadly of his water bill. On the knob of the faucet he saw again a faded blue S. S, he thought, what the hell does S stand for? H hot, C cold. What the hell kind of faucet is S? Old clothes hung on a hook on the back of the door. A man's blue wash pants hung inside out, the zipper split like a peeled banana, the crowded concourse of seams at the crotch like carelessly sewn patches.

Everything is closing in on Greenspahn, who is at once impacted and trickling away like a faucet, heading towards ruin. Everything he cares about has either been taken from him or is now aligned maliciously against him. His store has been ravaged by thieves, his feckless son is dead, his manhood has peeled and split open like a banana, and his ability to read the world around him, to decode its signifiers in a coherent way, is gone. Even his one sacrosanct possession, his purity of mourning, is pried from his closed fist, his son emerging through the fog of repressed memory to reveal himself as yet another thief in a world of thieves. Hence Greenspahn's rages and rants are exposed for what they are: willful evasions of a truth to which he's had access all along. And so, like Lear, he must pay the ultimate price for his blindness—stripped of his armor and privileges, stumbling naked and friendless through the storm.

Elkin's story is a bracing reminder that the music of Yiddish, or Yiddish-inflected English, is itself a marvelous vehicle for rants. Implicit in the sound and syntax of the language is a sort of nervous irony, half-playful, half-critical, that can't seem to let well enough alone. It's always fiddling with itself. *Self, shmelf.* And once it starts with the fiddling, once that Catskills conga line really gets going with the *shmos* and the *shmendricks*, the *shmucks* and the *shlemiehls* and the *shlimazels*, there's no stopping. Yiddish, the linguists tell us, was originally "*teytsh*," which translates to "language of people." In other words, popular speech. The voice of the lower classes, the bantering, storytelling voice of the street-smart, the embattled; those, in short, with a whole lot of shit to complain about. ("Complaint," says the poet Carl Dennis, "is one of the basic forms of spiritual expression"). Hence the relish, the visceral pleasure—you can feel it in the mouth, you can hear it in the ear—in all that poking fun and tearing down, that teasing, irreverent deconstruction of hoity-toity pretentious airs. Hence the *shtick*, the *shpiel*, the *kvetch*, the *shpritz*, the whole theatrical performance of humorous complaint, which spreads to the host country via Yiddish Theatre and its stepchild, vaudeville, and later finds its ultimate expression in standup comedy, where the noisy transmutation of alienation and pain are converted, in good Freudian fashion, into laughter and cash and the love of women.

The argument being, Yiddish and American English make a pretty nice fit. Both are mongrels at heart. Their energies are playful, improvisatory, making themselves up as they go along, combining high and low registers almost accidentally. We can see this at work in the breakthrough novels of Bellow and Malamud and Roth: their discovery that the voices of their childhoods and the high rhetoric of their literary forebears were not just compatible but also artistically and historically necessary, an unapologetic, free-form mode of expression for a new set of cultural realities. "I . . . go at things as I have taught myself, free-style, and will make the record in my own way," begins *Augie March*. ". . . Everybody knows there is no fineness or accuracy of suppression."

Philip Roth is another Jewish-American writer who, in attempting to jump from one side of the hyphen to the other—from the nice Jewish boy to the licentious, unbridled American—finds himself impaled on the very fence he hoped to surmount, and makes that howling pain both subject and fuel. Here's a characteristic passage from *Portnoy's Complaint*:

Look, am I exaggerating to think it's practically miraculous that I'm ambulatory? The hysteria and the superstition! The watch-its and be-carefuls! You mustn't do this, you can't do that—hold it! Don't you're breaking an important law! What law? Whose law? . . . I couldn't even contemplate drinking a glass of milk with my salami sandwich without giving serious offense to God Almighty. Imagine then what my conscience gave me for all that jerking off! The guilt, the fears—the terror bred into my bones! What in their world was not charged with danger, dripping with germs, fraught with peril? Oh, where was the gusto, where was the boldness and courage?

Portnoy's extended rant, which is to say the novel itself, is both a son's plaintive Oedipal cry and the liberating war-whoop of that wild Indigenous savage, the Id, against the Old World, civilized dictates of his conscience. It's not for nothing that Portnoy's father, like Elkin's Greenspahn, suffers from constipation: he too is "imprisoned" by his life circumstances as a salesman, a middle man, with ownership of his intestinal tract entirely "in the hands of the firm of Worry, Fear & Frustration." No wonder he can't let go. That Roth's first novel was called *Letting Go*, and was noteworthy for its lack of that very quality, for its moral equilibrium, its thorough, patient, judicious exploration of the compromises one makes along the road to maturity, was an irony the writer himself recognized all too well. It wasn't until he let go himself—stopped being the dutiful son, the decorous young graduate student of literature who studied that famously constipated great white father Henry James, and let fly with his own aggressive, parricidal instincts, that he became the messy brilliant writer he became, with an almost infinite capacity to appall us.

> Leave off with the blushing, bury the shame, you are no longer your mother's naughty little boy! Where appetite is concerned, a man in his thirties is responsible to no one but himself! That's what's so nice about growing up! You want to take? You take! Debauch a little bit, for Christ's sake! STOP DENYING YOURSELF! STOP DENYING THE TRUTH!

In the course of the book we watch Portnoy's rant accelerate—or degenerate—until at last it arrives at its terminal destination: a primal scream which, as Chekhov or a good therapist might say, and as the final (punch) line of the novel reminds us, is in fact only a beginning:

> It makes me want to *scream*, the ridiculous disproportion of the guilt! May I? Will that shake them up too much out in the waiting

room? Because that's maybe what I need most of all, to howl. A pure howl, without any more words between me and it! Aaaaaaaaaaaaaaa aaaaaaaaaaaaaaaaaaaaaaaaaaaaaaaaaaaaaaaaaaaaaaaaaaaaaaaaaaaaaaaaa aaaaaaaaaaaaaaaaaaaaaaaaaaaaaaaaaaaaaaaaaaaaaaaaaaaaaaaaaaaaaaaaa aaaaaaaaaaaaaaaaaaaaaaaaaaaaaaaaaaaaaaaaaaaaaaaaaaaaahhh!!!!

Arguably all rants, like all writers, aspire to this state of pure howling wordlessness, to slip the bonds of language for good and engage with the dark, unfathomable mess below. The paradoxical inadequacy of language to get beyond itself, the futility of the head as it tries to detach itself from the body—perhaps these work best as comic premises, as occasions for bad jokes. The salt the writer rubs his or her wounds in, reveling in the discomfort. And taking notes.

Still, Portnoy's issues are nothing new. They're not even particularly Jewish. To feel squeezed into conventional categories from which you yearn to break free—but not *too* free, not so free that you can't recognize yourself or be recognized by your people, who drive you crazy—is not just Portnoy's complaint but America's, the source of our greatest rants and art. Think of Ellison's Invisible Man, listening to the blues in his underground hole. Or Percival Everett's novel *Erasure*, which is less a meditation on Black invisibility as on the invisibility of the contemporary, Ellison-influenced Black writer. Like Portnoy, Everett's novel is composed as an extended screed, an angry protest against that philistine perception that wants to box the ethnic writer into a corner, and keep him there. Here's Percy's Complaint in a nutshell:

> I stood in the middle of Border's thinking how much I hated the chain and chains like it. I'd talked to too many owners of little, real bookstores who were being driven to the poorhouse by what they called the WalMart of books. I decided to see if the store had any of my books, firm in my belief that even if they did, my opinion about them would be unchanged. I went to Literature and did not see me. I went to Contemporary Fiction and did not find me, but when I fell back a couple of steps I found a section called African-American Studies and there, arranged alphabetically and neatly, read *undisturbed*, were four of my books including my *Persians* of which the only thing ostensibly African-American was my jacket photograph. I became quickly irate, my pulse speeding up, my brow furrowing... that fucking store was taking food from my table.

"I went to Literature and did not see *me*"—a nightmare of invisibility that all writers recognize and experience at some point. Like going to the mirror and not finding your face.

Speaking of invisibility, where are the women writers here, anyway? Where's Jean Rhys, Jamaica Kincaid, Kathy Acker, Flannery O'Connor, Lorrie Moore?[1] "Women are supposed to be very calm generally," writes Charlotte Brontë, "but women feel just as men feel." True. And yet no less an arbiter than Virginia Woolf worries, in that brilliant if rather decorous rant, *A Room of One's Own*, that Brontë's books "will be deformed and twisted. She will write in a rage where she should write calmly. She will write foolishly where she should write wisely. She will write of herself where she should write of her characters." Would anyone say this, or even *think* it, about Lawrence or Dostoevsky? And if not, what does *that* suggest? That women writers are held, or hold themselves—think of Jane Austen covering her manuscripts with blotting paper—to a higher standard of decorum or artfulness than men? Or simply a different one? "It would be a thousand pities if women wrote like men," Woolf says.

And herein lies the problem of the female ranter, for whom both the access to rage, and the expression of it, has historically been filtered through a more complex screen. In Jamaica Kincaid's work, we sense a *withheld* rant against her characters' very voicelessness, against a whole world in which one's face is not allowed to show up in the mirror. Her repetitive, somnolent rhythms are like the seiche left behind by an explosion—a furious but expanding near-silence. Her narrators' consciousness of their own powerlessness, their irritable compulsion to assign and then refuse to assign blame, before assigning blame all over again, results in a smoldering litany of sub-verbal feelings over which they can't help pouring gasoline, as in this passage from *At the Bottom of the River*:

> I walk over to the fireplace. Standing in front of the fireplace, I try to write my name in the dead ashes with my big toes. I cannot write my name in the dead ashes with my big toes. My big toes, now dirty, I try to clean by rubbing it vigorously on a clean royal-blue rug. The royal-blue rug now has a dark spot, and my big toes has a strong burning sensation. Oh, sensation. I am filled with sensation. I

---

1. And by the way while we're at it, where's Leslie Jamison, Rebecca Traister, Melissa Febos, Samantha Irby, Patricia Lockwood, and countless other contemporary writers who have been navigating, forcefully and eloquently, this red-hot moment for the investigation and literary expression of female rage? That this essay predates them, and is already way too long as it is, makes name-checking them here an inadequate but necessary addendum.

feel—oh, how I feel. I feel, I feel, I feel. I have no words right now for how I feel.

Kincaid's impatience with language, and her fiery and intemperate self-regard, are features Lawrence for one would recognize and identify with. Does she "write of herself where she should write of her characters"? And in so doing, is she writing more "like men," or less? And are these distinctions even valuable or interesting at this point, let alone makeable by a person of my particular gender? Listen, I'm as tremulous in the face of female rage as the next man. The refusal to demur at this point should of course be viewed (and licensed) in light of the long oppressive history of enforced demurral trailing behind it.

In short, the rant of the female writer is both implicitly and explicitly political. This can lead to some excesses of its own, as in Sylvia Plath for instance, whose oft-quoted "Daddy," by blurring the lines between Oedipal rage and the horrors of fascism—

I thought every German was you.
And the language obscene
An engine, an engine,
Chuffing me off like a Jew.
A Jew to Dachau, Auschwitz, Belsen.
I began to talk like a Jew.
I think I may well be a Jew.

manages to remain "so entangled in biographical circumstances and rampages so permissively in the history of other people's sorrows"—I am quoting Seamus Heaney here, but it's hardly a unique response—"that it simply overdraws its rights to our sympathy." And that's putting it mildly. Plath's poem, for all its brilliance, is also in both ethical and aesthetic terms a cheap high, its conflation of images not just too much but borderline obscene. And yet it's a hell of a rant.

Don DeLillo's febrile and obsessive rock 'n' roll novel, *Great Jones Street*, features one Bucky Wunderlick, another Molloy-like narrator in retreat, trying to withdraw "to that unimprinted level where all sound is silken and nothing erodes in the mad weather of language." The irony of the novel and the source of its energy are the way Bucky's repudiating silence provides a still center around which every other character (and the author himself) weaves baroque verbal arabesques that more often than not take the shape of rants. Here's his manager, Globke, whose aggressive rhythms and vulgarity make him sound like a refugee from a Roth novel:

41

My whole life is a study in bad taste. Bad taste is the foundation for every success I've ever had. I'm a self-made mogul in an industry that abounds in bad taste. Look at me. Mogul is written all over me. How did I get there? Aggressiveness got me there. Massive double-dealing. Loudmouthedness. Insults beyond belief. Little white lies. Farts and belches. Betraying a friend and then bragging about it. These are the things that give you stature in the industry. Not just respect or clout or notability. Stature. It's not enough to betray a friend. That gives you respect at the very most. You have to supply the extra touch. You betray a friend and then you brag about it. That's star quality. That gives you stature.

Among the most startling observations to make about Globke's rant, about Lawrence's, about Portnoy's and Molloy's and the drunken guy in the Waits song, is also the most obvious: that they don't seem to care if we're *listening* to them. They're too intoxicated with their own fermented juices, too high on their own supply, to pay attention to *us*. Their heedless-ness and obliviousness is what's wrong with them, but it's also the source of their power. The inner need is so great, the inner voice so loud, that they've lost all sight of the membrane between themselves and the world. And so they stalk a labyrinth of their own construction, a hall of mirrors in which it's impossible to see past their own head.

All of which makes them weirdly honest, even rather innocent report-ers on the self and the world. Neurologists say the limbic system, which drives those organic functions over which we can never achieve conscious control (hunger, sexual desire, inspiration), is wired more intricately to the temporal lobes than any other region of the cortex. This suggests, among other things, that the writer's maniacal mood swings, along with the dark cognitive sediment they dislodge, are both byproducts of creativ-ity and its source.

Well, one can only hope. Sitting at the desk, trying to pound together a little fictive furniture and wheel it into place, there's an increasing sense, as the hours pass, that one is engaged in the very quotidian labor one became a writer to avoid: that slow, methodical *and then, and then*, along with an equal-and-opposite suspicion that none of this, in the end, really quite matters. Even as we narrow in on our story, our story seems to be narrowing us: limiting our vision, our range of possibilities. Perhaps our characters experience this too. Every door we open before them means that others are de facto closed. This makes us all a little crazy. We're all sitting alone at a desk drinking way too much coffee, turning sentences inside out and upside down, with a growing sense of shame and time-wasting, and meanwhile our characters are just trapped there waiting to *do* something. But what? It's impossible to know, trapped as we are in the maze of our limitations. Only words to play with. Honestly the thing about creative work is that the appeal of going on with it is rarely all that much greater than the appeal of not going on with it. The challenge is to go from whining about this state of affairs to feeding off of it. Letting fly. We rant because we can't achieve the ease and fluency of our dreams, our characters rant because ditto, our novels rant because ditto, and maybe instead of repressing or containing that frustration we should attend to it, maybe even accentuate it, just *blow the bloody doors off* and ride that rough beast over the horizon, into a darkness whose parameters we can't begin to measure.

When you get right down to it, the self has only the one plaintive and repetitive song to sing, with a very limited set of variations. *I want! I want! I want!* hollers Bellow's Henderson. *Not me. Not me. Not me*, sings Waits' drunkard. "*You have no idea what it's like to be me*," shrieks Peter Lorre's *M.* "*Who is it*," cries Lear, "*that can tell me who I am?*" Any way you phrase it there's a volcanic force of passion and linguistic power in there, waiting to be tapped. A shedding of the vestments of self, an exponential growth in feeling. When the husk of personality is crushed, who knows what wondrous depths of the heart may be exposed?

Possibly going to extremes has never required getting there: the attempt, the possibility of attempt, may be enough. It's not much of a comfort but one can live with it. Maybe the only peace we can achieve is a provisional peace, a fighter's peace, with the Me that longs not to be Me. But is. But is.

Elkin

❦

Though I have read pretty much everything he ever wrote, and think and talk about the man all the time, I met Stanley Elkin only once, in 1992. He was visiting Cambridge. A dinner party had been arranged, and though I was new in town I was invited because he had given my first novel a nice blurb and apparently either wanted to meet me or consented to do so out of politeness. Politeness! I'd read enough of his work to know better. Politeness was not Elkin's thing. Candor was his thing. Rudeness was his thing. The rage and wit and pressure of consciousness against that frail bag of bones, the body, that was his thing. ("A captive's captive," he writes in *A Bad Man*. "It's no joke, it costs to live.") He roared into the room in his wheelchair, a shrewd, tough Jew, ready for commotion. People were milling around, talking about trips they'd either just taken or would take soon. Elkin would have none of it. Or rather, he'd have *all* of it. "How fucking great it must be to be ambulatory!" he hollered. "Why don't you all just shut up." If this was shtick, it wasn't *only* shtick: he really meant it. And why shouldn't he? We were upstairs at the Harvard Faculty Club, the china shop to end all china shops. There were distinguished literary people eager to meet him. Seamus Heaney was seated to Elkin's left; the poor man had to keep diving under the table to retrieve Elkin's cutlery, which he did with great good humor, even after Elkin began with the kibitzing about how overrated Joyce was. "All that moo-cow shit," he said, "how do you stand it?" Joan was across the table, lovely and bemused; I had the sense that many of the outrageous things he said that night were for her benefit, to make her laugh. And she laughed a lot.

Meanwhile Elkin looked awful. His color was poor, his hands shook, his lids were melting and droopy. Otherwise, though of course I had nothing to compare it with, he seemed in pretty good form. At some point in the dinner he appeared to make the decision to go ahead and eat and let other people say things for a while, though you could see he'd have preferred not to. Then at last the coffee came, and he turned to me.

"Liked your book," he said, in a tone that could just as well have meant he hated it, or never even read it, for all I knew. His eyes were shining and intent, not entirely devoid of malice. "So let me ask you something."

I nodded shyly. On some level I'd been waiting for this question, it occurred to me, my entire adult life. The man was the greatest writer I'd ever personally sat next to at a dinner table, and whatever he was about to ask or say about my novel would, I felt sure, represent a serious and formidable response, one that would penetrate deep into the heart of my work, such as it was, and perhaps even that other, seemingly lesser affair, my life, such as *it* was. So I leaned forward, sitting on my hands to keep them from trembling.

"What kind of rent you pay?"

Someone barked out a laugh. It may have been Joan, it may have been Elkin; for all I know it may have been me.

"You don't want to know," I said.

"Sure I do."

I told him what I paid for rent. He was appalled. I was too.

We went on to talk for a while about the hardships and indignities, not all of them economic, of quotidian life. Then Elkin grew tired. The skin on his face slackened; it looked even more pallid and papery than when he'd come in. He hollered abruptly to Joan across the table that it was time to go, and she got up at once and wheeled him out of the room. A year or two later he died. I no longer paid rent by then, I'd bought a house, a small one, with a lot of things wrong with it, and a yard notable principally for its confinements. The price of that too was appalling. But as a master once wrote, it costs to live.

Ain't That Pretty at All,

Or Going to the Tigers

One day back in grad school my advisor, a savvy and successful novelist whose books meant a great deal to me, whom I had just gone five grand into debt and traveled three thousand miles to work with, called me into his office and sat me down to talk about the chapter I had submitted from my novel in progress. His expression was purposeful, intense; he seemed eager to get down to business. Clearly the work I'd submitted had impressed him in some particular way, elevated me a little from the other surly, miserable students in the workshop. I could all but feel him weighing the manuscript in his hand, as if deliberating how much postage to apply when he sent it to his agent.

"Look," he said, and I did, at a piece of parchment bond paper so capillaried with red marks it might have been the face of a stroke victim, "cut the crap, okay? Enough with these F. Scott Fitzgerald sentences."

This was, on one level, the nicest, most fulsome compliment the man would ever give me. After all it was my love for Fitzgerald and his sentences that had inspired me to write in the first place. If every writer, as Saul Bellow once claimed, is a reader moved to emulation (and my advisor wasn't so hot on Bellow's sentences either), then to be accused of writing the kinds of sentences that had made me want to write those kinds of sentences? On one level it was very nice to hear.

Unfortunately my advisor didn't mean it on that level. He meant it on a different level, a lower level. He meant that being enthralled as I was to lovely, thrilling, Daisy Buchanan-ish prose was an infatuation I had to grow out of fast, lest my work wind up face-down in an abandoned pool. He himself was a rough-and-tumble realist, streety and sharp—a Redskin, in Philip Rahv's famous phrase. Already he had me pegged as a member of that wan lesser tribe, the Palefaces, those cerebral, overly refined aesthetes who hung out in cafes, reading French poetry and doodling precious *bon mots* in overpriced notebooks. *Moi!* That this judgment was ludicrously unfair, presumptuous, and reductive did not make it, alas, any less true. I hurried out of his office that day like the kid in Joyce's "Araby," the soft underbelly of my assumptions exposed, my face burning, my hands clenched, shadow-boxing with shame.

All of which took place many years ago now. Just another once-humiliating, now-comic anecdote one shares with one's peers over a shit-load of drinks, the Paleface equivalent of a war story. In other words, though I often refer to it, I don't often think about it.

But maybe I should. Because there arrives a point in every vocation where the efficacy of one's long-distance path through the dark woods of Time comes into question, where it becomes necessary to consider the choices one has made—whether or not one is aware of having made them—along the way. An interlude of mid-career self-scrutiny, in which all the old, now-calcified assumptions are held up against the light and examined for flaws. What would we change, if we had the chance?

Like most people, I would often prefer to be someone else. Ideally, the prose this other self would write would not be like mine at all. This other self would not write lyrical and elongated sentences that unfurl like a garden hose, spritzing dewily over every bush, thorn, and flower. No, the prose of this other person would be coiled and sharp, deadly as a snake. But here's the thing: you can't just *choose* to be a snake. There are issues of temperament involved. Of culture and nurture. Arguably, to be Jewish, for example, is to incline, more or less from Eden onward, less toward snakes than snake *victims*. With a few notable exceptions (Babel, Mailer, Mamet) Jewish writers tend towards the indoor, the psychological, the Paleface; they lack that mind of winter, that cold equipment, that steely, scrupulous will to violence we see in Flannery O'Connor, Robert Stone, Cormac McCarthy, and the other Catholic Redskins. Then too there are limits to our stylistic elasticity. The rubber band of sensibility can only stretch so far. Even the most strenuous reexamination of our own linguistic patterns is conducted within the confines of those patterns, the patterns of those patterns. You can wind up feeling encircled by funhouse mirrors, unable to see beyond the freakishly elongated reflections of your own head.

Nonetheless: it's important to try to get past our own heads, which, however busy and capacious, can only take us so far. The same is true of literary style. "As you get older," says Thomas McGuane, a recovering "word drunk" by his own admission,

> you should get impatient with showing off in literature. It is easier to settle for blazing light than to find a language for the real. Whether you are a writer or a bird-dog trainer, life should winnow the super-

fluous language. The real thing should become plain. You should go straight to what you know best. . . . You want something that is drawn like a bow, and a bow is a simple instrument. A good writer should get a little bit cleaner and probably a little bit plainer as life and the oeuvre go on.

For all its plain good sense, this strikes me as a fairly radical take. Most young artists resist imperatives and prescriptions; they don't like being told what's real and true, let alone what they should or shouldn't do about it. But McGuane's "winnowing down" is the product of a longer view of time, a moral and aesthetic response to the realities of middle age, that war of attrition. The shadow of all those attended funerals may not change what he chooses to write about, but it changes how he sees, and how he writes too. There's no equivocating here, no epistemological dithering about how terms like "truth" and "the real" are just silly premodern arti-facts tarnished by years of rough treatment by lawyers, politicians, and humanities professors with French surnames. No, the writer's outlook is stony and clear, absolute. If experience—or let's just go ahead and say *death*—teaches us what's real and what isn't, then to pretend otherwise, whether in substance or style, is a cowardly evasion, a shirking of the writ-er's fundamental responsibility to find words that distill conditions of being. The rest is just so much commentary scribbled in the margins.

"In the beginner's mind there are many possibilities," goes the Zen teaching, "in the expert's few."

Another expression of this can be seen in a late essay by Natalia Ginz-burg, "My Vocation":

We are adult because we have behind us the silent presence of the dead, whom we ask to judge our current actions and from whom we ask forgiveness for past offences . . . we are adult because of that brief moment when one day it fell to our lot to live when we had looked at the things of the world as if for the last time, when we had renounced our possession of them and returned them to the will of God: and suddenly the things of the world appeared to us in their just place be-neath the sky, and the human beings too. In that brief moment we found a point of equilibrium for our wavering life, and it seemed to us that we could . . . find there the words for our vocation.

This same "language for the real," this winnowing directness, under-lies and often *over*lies the work of Chekhov. His lyric effects, if we can even call them that, are dispensed sparely but tactically, like a Japanese meal. They never leave the page bloated; they hit a quick, distinct flavor note and then flit back to the kitchen with a delicate grace, a pellucid lightness of manner, that's both an artistic and (if his letters are any indication) behavioral ideal. "You may weep and moan over your stories, you may suffer together with your heroes," he tells one correspondent, "but I consider one must do this so that the reader does not notice it. The more objective, the stronger will be the effect." That there's no such thing as "objective" writing—that literary prose is always a manipulated impression, a trick of subjective light—is too obvious a point to bother over. It's how to *achieve* that impression without looking like you're trying to achieve it, how to walk that high wire without sweating, that obsesses Chekhov. His style is a kind of anti-style, its effects arising casually, indirectly, often prosaically. "He goes to parties," observes Nabokov, "clad in his everyday suit . . . the juicy verb, the hothouse adjective, the crème de menthe epithet, these were foreign to him." This is meant as a compliment, though another critic, D. S. Mirsky, manages to turn it into an indictment: "He has no feeling for words. No Russian writer of anything like his significance used a language so devoid of all raciness and nerve."

Not being schooled in Russian, I'm in no position to judge the relative stupidity of this remark. Does it matter? Yes, Chekhov's vocabulary is deliberately plain, and deploys few ostentatious or even particularly interesting metaphors and similes. But his scorn for the lyrical, like a former smoker's scorn for a patch, is as knowing as it is severe. It's as if lyricism is a bad habit he's forever struggling to put behind him for good. Oh, it still rears its head occasionally. When he lifts his gaze, say, from the small muddle of human affairs to the vast, impersonal landscape around them, his most expansive, full-throated prose comes forth, layered with the sort of subtle musical patterns and cadences and manipulative use of repetition, pauses, and ellipses we might just as well call lyrical. And yet it's felicities remain lightly worn. The beauty arises not despite his lack of interest in beauty, other than to note how transient and insubstantial it is, but because of it. Beautiful, not beautiful—in Chekhov these and all such binaries are exposed as facile and irrelevant, vaguely vulgar. Things are never either/or, but both/and. When Gurov, the snobby cold-fish protagonist of "Lady and the Pet Dog," spots Anna Sergeyevna at the opera, something fateful happens: all of a sudden the straight, conventional lines that have separated his public affairs from his private ones begin to blur into a dreamy, dissolute haze:

She, this little, undistinguished woman, lost in a provincial crowd, with a vulgar lorgnette in her hand, filled his whole life now, was his sorrow and his joy, the only happiness that he now desired for himself, and to the sounds of the bad orchestra, of the miserable local violins, he thought how lovely she was. He thought and dreamed.

Note that pride of place goes to the sorrow, not the joy, as the thought gives way to the dream. For Chekhov, the breakdown of the simple into the binary, and the binary into the atomic, is at once a catastrophic and redemptive process, unwelcome but inevitable. ("Of course all life," Fitzgerald observes in *The Crack-Up*, "is a process of breaking down.") To discover that each moment, when it arrives, is no longer simply itself, solo and unencumbered, but comes freighted with cumbersome bags of memory, loss, and regret . . . this is the wisdom of maturity, a wisdom most of us would prefer to do without. If Gurov's surrender to the dream-drift of the irrational leads to a version (or inversion) of McGuane's "plain winnowed truth," it's a very swampy, messy truth, as mysterious and destabilizing as thunder in winter. That this truth can only be experienced, not explained, imposes its own stylistic demands on the writer. The clever, high-concept satire of the early work no longer obtains. His own breezy advice—"Write what you like. If you haven't facts, make up with lyricism"—is now useless to him, a fossil of another era, a glib certainty long outgrown.

The conflict between lived facts and imposed lyricism can also be viewed in grammatical terms: as a tug-of-war between adjective and noun. The lyric writer's affinity and/or weakness for the adjective is at once endearingly earnest and embarrassingly insistent. It represents a kind of religious faith—first in the power of the adjective to do right by a specific noun, and second and more broadly, in the ability of language to do right by *its* noun (reality, I mean) in all its latent and subordinate depths. The modern writer tends to be a skeptic, if not a diehard atheist, in that particular church. ("The total and unique adjective," Robbe-Grillet snorts, "which attempts to unite all the inner qualities, the entire hidden soul of things.") Or maybe it's the other way around. Maybe it's a *lack* of faith, a frantic insecurity about language's ability to adhere to the real, that inspires some writers to press too much of it upon the page, like a stoned teenager Scotch-taping the unruly corners of a Hendrix poster to his bedroom wall. Either way the stuff won't quite stick. Even as we struggle to affix language to the world, we only manage to obscure it, fogging up the window with the huff and puff of our own breath.

Point being, a tendency to render something in a manner that foregrounds the rendering, not the something, can get old fast. Reading a novel that feels overly protracted and finessed makes us antsy, peevish. Enough with the light show, we think, enough with the incense, the dry ice, the elaborate riddles and evasions. No wonder people hate novels. They really are just *words*, aren't they? True, we like words, up to a point. We like a narrative voice that's fluent, shapely, resonant, neatly symbolic. But what happens when we apply that same voice to material that isn't shapely or fluent in the least? That's at war in fact with shapeliness and fluency, at war with neatness, at war with reason itself? Something like this is what happens:

> Amid the glittering impassivity of the many buildings across the East River, an empty spot had appeared, as if by electronic command, beneath the sky that, but for the sulfurous cloud streaming south toward the ocean, was pure blue, rendered uncannily pristine by the absence of jet trails.

Reading this honeyed prose, with its wealth of adjectives, its fine, discriminating clauses, the brain-stem is curiously soothed if not pampered and lulled. On the other hand, *should* we be soothed? Should reading about the sky over downtown Manhattan on September 12, 2001 be a honeyed experience? You could be forgiven for wondering if the writer in this case (John Updike) has purposely set out to parody, or exemplify, or maybe reaffirm the very cultural privileges and insulations now under attack. Whether the result is a political statement, or a willful denial of politics, or both, it feels wrong. You want to call in the Reality Police. You want the Truth. You want to *hurt*.

(It's instructive to compare the passage above to Don DeLillo's account of the same aftermath—"There is something empty in the sky." A line that registers the shock of absence with stunning efficiency. Or Hemingway's Frederic Henry looking down at his wounded leg and thinking, "My knee wasn't there." What other words need be said?)

At such times, we may well turn with relief to the noun. The thing. The solid, seemingly reliable object. Nouns are modest by nature; they make few claims on our emotions, request no special treatment or favors. Next to the noun's rugged, Gary Cooper-ish laconicism, the adjective can look sweaty and undignified, like Peter Lorre in *Casablanca*, pleading for special favors it hasn't earned. We're tempted to step away, wipe the stain of its corruptions off our sleeve, and get on with our business. *Clear this away*, says the overseer of the hunger artist's limp, useless corpse. Give us the real thing, the panther, vivid and unmediated. Show us his claws.

And yet even real-thingness, taken to its extreme—did someone say

Robbe-Grillet?—can begin to seem a bit fancy, a bit fussy and mannered in its own way. Think of the difference between good Hemingway and bad Hemingway ("Down at the station there were five whores waiting for the train to come in, and six white men and four Indians.") The materiality of the noun can turn stolid, unyielding, its very laconicism sentimental. Not all plainspoken people are interesting. A lot of them are just plain. And who wants that?

Which is only to say that whichever direction you take, you can wind up in pretty much the same place. You say *tomato*, I say *red round seed-spilling fruit*; what matters is the conviction of the observation, and the musical intensity of its voice. The concrete implies the abstract, the simple implies the complex, and vice versa. Even McGuane's candor and directness, his hostility to rhetorical posturing, is itself (he'd likely be first to concede) a kind of rhetorical posture, not plain at all.

If every style is an argument with its own opposite, its shadow, its fraternal twin, whether the terms of the argument should evolve over time is a question we're all likely to answer, as McGuane does, in the affirmative. But how? For every major artist whose later works calcify into mannerism, there are a thousand minor ones who never even make it *that* far. After all, we have only so many arrows in our quiver. To take up other weapons, and hit the target again and again, is no easy thing. And that's not taking into account the demands of a marketplace where brand recognition is everything, where a fixed if not static "signature style" is a valuable if not necessary asset. Even the famously uncompromising Mark Rothko, according to his biographer, made a conscious choice in mid-career to give the world more or less what it wanted from him. And what did it want? It wanted "Rothkos." It wanted ineffable hovering rectangles of color, and *more* ineffable hovering rectangles of color, not a set of doodly, semi-surrealist multiforms no one knew what to make of. And so the artist who begins by laying siege to pre-cut frames and reducing them to splinters, eventually sues for peace, and frames himself.

Not that most of us wouldn't sign that treaty in a heartbeat, and with our own blood. After all, we tell ourselves, it's an achievement just to go on *doing* this stuff, even if the stuff we're doing bears a suspicious resemblance to the stuff we've already done. Not everyone is a bloody fucking genius. But just for argument's sake, what might a mature, *non*-signature style by a bloody fucking genius look like?

Edward Said, in his unfinished but influential *On Late Style*, finds in the late works of Beethoven, Strauss, Lampedusa, Visconti, and Thomas Mann not McGuane's plainspoken, winnowed-down "real" thing but something like the opposite: a landscape of "intransigence, difficulty, and unresolved contradiction." Said is out to interrogate, as they say, the whole notion of maturity, and not just in the arts. What if age *doesn't* yield the serene perspective of "ripeness is all"? What if instead of harmony and resolution we find only "a sort of deliberately unproductive productiveness," a "devotion to the truth of unreconciled relations"? What if our apprehension of the real is undermined by a growing awareness that reality itself—the *self* itself—is shot through with holes? If so, then perhaps some new, messier vocabulary is necessary. "A catching fire between extremes," Adorno calls it, "which no longer allow for any secure middle ground. In the history of art," he concludes, "late works are the catastrophes."

Death in Venice, though hardly a late work for Mann, reads like a very late work for *man*. We all know the story: Aschenbach, a highly accomplished artist, a man given to fastidious brooding in expensive rooms, arrives in Venice at a creative impasse, his ends out of synch with his means. As the narrator coolly observes, "His work had ceased to be marked by that fiery play of fancy which is the product of joy." And so to Venice, "that wild, presumably unrestrained region where desires are realized and fantasies fulfilled." Aschenbach, like a Paul Bowles character, like all such imperialists, wants to gain something for nothing and then make good his escape. He craves the heat of the orgy, as Norman Mailer used to say, but not its murder. "*He would go on a journey*," he tells himself, "*Not far—not all the way to the tigers*." But in the end the tigers get him anyway. The ever-receding ideal of beauty embodied by his homoerotic fixation, Tadzio, leads him deep into a darkness and disorder from which there is no possibility of return. Like Gurov, he's so bored with his own detachment, his halfway measures and patterned, systemic ways, that he deliberately, miserably, ecstatically succumbs to something larger and more powerful, shedding all hard-won qualities of mind, will, discipline—all the tools of a culture fighting off its discontents—along the way. "The hostility to civilization," Freud reminds us, "is produced by the pressure that civilization exercises, the renunciations of instinct which it demands." And so with Aschenbach. In the end, he blows his top—spewing the hot, spasmodic stream that is his genuine, if latent, self—and collapses in an ashen heap, truly spent.

If Venice seems an apt staging ground for this apocalyptic drama, that may be because it's not ground per se at all, but a kind of swampy hybrid, a geographical and imaginative interzone. Land and water, east and west, north and south . . . in Venice, the beauties of Paradise and the corruptions of the Inferno are inextricably twined. With its bad smells, gorgeous art, and crumbling walls, *over*-ripeness is all. Solid things perch precariously above the sea, as if secretly longing to merge with it, to lose definition in the heat and then trickle away like so much runny hair dye. Prominent among these melting forms is Mann's own shapely, cerebral style, which like a lot of modernist art seems to revel in the spectacle of its own destruction. As Aschenbach puts it, speaking for both himself and his creator:

> Our magisterial style is all folly and pretence, our honourable repute a farce, the crowd's belief in us is merely laughable. And to teach youth, or the populace, by means of art is a dangerous practice and ought to be forbidden. For what good can an artist be as a teacher, when from his birth up he is headed direct for the pit? We may want to shun it and attain to honour in the world; but however we turn, it draws us still. So, then, since knowledge might destroy us, we will have none of it. For knowledge, Phaedrus, does not make him who possesses it dignified or austere. Knowledge is all-knowing, understanding, forgiving; it takes up no position, sets no store by form. It has compassion with the abyss-it is the abyss.

What if knowledge and form, in other words, don't play so well together after all? Say that artists' obsession with beauty does not make them wiser and more dignified with age, but increasingly vulnerable to the intoxications of desire and despair, increasingly prone "not to excellence but to excess." In the war between beauty and pride, beauty, that blue angel, always wins. What good is pride anyway? In the long run it's a non-sustainable fuel; sooner or later the wells run dry. We may as well learn to do without it now, strip it away, expose ourselves to the murk below. As Aschenbach groans, with a certain helpless excitement, "We cannot pull ourselves together, we can only fall apart." A point with which Fitzgerald would reluctantly agree.

John Cheever, who knew a thing or two about stripping down, has some penetrating passages about Fitzgerald in his journals, which double as reflections upon certain tendencies of his own:

> The writer cultivates, extends, raises and inflates his imagination, sure that this is his destiny, his usefulness, his contribution to the understanding of good and evil. As he inflates his imagination, he inflates his capacity for anxiety, and inevitably becomes the victim

of crushing phobias that can only be allayed by lethal doses of heroin or alcohol.

Anxiety for Cheever is yet another form of excessive beauty, another spark thrown off by the imagination's lonely, maddening, ever-grinding wheel. To write, after all, one must sit alone in a room for many hours, mumbling to oneself and conjuring "plots." How closely this practice resembles mental illness—or yields to it—is something we prefer not to think about.

But how can we help thinking about it, when we confront the late, deliriously involuted work of a Melville, a James, a Woolf, a Joyce? Here the trajectory over the years is not a paring down but a ramping up, a fidgety, groping prodigiousness, an ornate and often wildly arcane laughter in the dark. (In his final plays and stories Beckett takes this, as he takes almost everything, to the zero point, if not beyond). A friend likens the experience of listening to late Mahler to watching a man pour gravy not just over the meat but over the potatoes, the green beans, the salad, the cake, and the table and floor too. You'd think a man would get sick of all that gravy. But suppose the only way he has to express that sickness is by means of, well, gravy?

No wonder when asked what he planned to do after *Finnegans Wake*, Joyce is said to have replied, "I think I'll write something very simple and short." All that work and isolation makes Jimmy a restless boy. If solitude, as Montaigne writes in his essays, gives birth to what's original in us, "it also gives birth to the opposite: to the perverse, the illicit, the absurd." To quiet that dissonance the writer may turn to alcohol, or drugs, or extracurricular affairs, or the ritual anaesthetic of compulsive work, or in Cheever's case all of the above. But these are no solutions. Maybe it's better, in the end, just to turn up the noise.

God knows maturity, in art as in life, is rarely in any conventional sense attractive. The saggy flesh, the wild eyebrows, those unruly ear and nose hairs and runaway moles... no, let's face it, maturity ain't that pretty at all. Shakespeare knows this: he and his characters grow increasingly less felicitous as his career goes on, their diction wilder, more concentrated, more obscure. "It is as if, having achieved age, they want none of its ... amiability or official ingratiation," Said writes. "Yet in none of them is mortality denied or evaded, but keeps coming back as the theme of death which undermines, and strangely elevates their uses of language and the aesthetic."

55

For a writer entirely allergic to ingratiation and embarrassment, take the much-remarked-upon late period Philip Roth. Mickey Sabbath's credo—"the unknown about any excess is how excessive it's been"—could as well apply to any Roth hero dating back to Portnoy. So it's with some surprise that one turns to his debut, *Goodbye, Columbus*, and discovers the lovely, fastidiously lyrical prose style, full of Jamesian discretion and restraint, that the writer would later go on to triumphantly shed:

> Once I'd driven out of Newark, past Irvington and the packed-in tangle of railroad crossings, switchmen shacks, lumberyards, Dairy Queens, and used-car lots, the night grew cooler. It was, in fact, as though the hundred and eighty feet that the suburbs rose in altitude above Newark brought one closer to heaven, for the sun itself became bigger, lower, and rounder, and soon I was driving past long lawns which seemed to be twirling water on themselves, and past houses where no one sat on stoops, where lights were on but no windows open, for those inside, refusing to share the very texture of life with those of us outside, regulated with a dial the amounts of moisture that were allowed access to their skin.

For comparison, consider a sentence from the scabrous, often brilliant *Sabbath's Theater*, written three and a half decades later:

> He was now six short years from seventy: what had him grasping at the broadening buttocks as though the tattooist Time had ornamented neither of them with its comical festoonery was his knowing inescapably that the game was just about over.

Whatever else you want to say about this sentence—and boy, where do you start?—it appears to have left all lyricism and shapeliness, all niceties of style, in the rear view. If anything it's a declaration of war on such things. Fuck niceties and style! Fuck lyricism and shapeliness! Who has *time* to be charming? Not Sabbath, and not Roth either. The prose flies open like a zipper and plunges heedlessly down the page, freeing itself from the constraints of good taste, good writing, good behavior. The novel itself, to switch metaphors, is no local; it's an express train, rattling and shrieking down memory's dark tunnel to the terminal, the last station.

Only in the final section do we understand that it's in this very direction—the graveyard—we've been headed all along. In that waning, retrospective light, the sexual chaos and slapstick that came before take on the sweetness of a ripe fruit, one that intensifies in taste even as it rots. Because it rots. Here, in the roaring, bravura elegy with which this utterly exhausting novel concludes, Sabbath's Lear-like loneliness, his Aschenbachian fever, burns through the scrim and torches the set. "And now, thought Sabbath, the feature attraction, the thing that matters most, the unforeseen culmination for which he had battled all his life. He had not realized how very long he'd been longing to be put to death."

Roth's willingness to pare down, hurry up, and uglify his prose stands in direct contrast to a writer like Updike, say, who continues to sustain, even in his last months, much of the same stately, pointillist, unfailingly lyrical density as before. Whether such admirable consistency represents a triumph or a failure of style is a question we could and probably should argue about. *Must* there be some palpable shift or disjunction, some greater sense of grit in the paint? Said would say yes.

"Late style," he writes, "is what happens if art does not abdicate its rights in favor of reality.

> It has the power to render disenchantment and pleasure without resolving the contradiction between them. What holds them in tension, as equal forces straining in opposite directions, is the artist's mature subjectivity, stripped of hubris and pomposity, unashamed either of its fallibility or of the modest assurance it has gained as a result of age and exile.

Of course, there's no shortage of unembarrassable old coots in the other arts as well. Wandering through the Musée Picasso in Paris, for example, it's impossible not to be struck by the amazing, lurid ugliness of the late works. If you don't believe me, here's the last portrait from 1972, called, appropriately enough, *Self Portrait Facing Death* (see p. 58).

This is as vivid an example of "Age masquerading as Juvenility" (as Hardy says of Father Time) as we're ever likely to find. Shakespeare too likes to have it both ways, his characters defying time's ravages even as they resign themselves to them: "Yet do thy worst, old Time; despite thy wrong / My love shall in my verse ever live young." And there's a similar stylistic response in the Virginia Woolf of *The Waves*. "Mrs. Woolf has not only passed up superficial reality; she has also passed up psychological reality," the *Times* reviewer concluded, half-admiringly and half-not. "She is not really concerned in 'The Waves' with people, she is hardly concerned in the prosaic sense with humanity: she is only concerned with the symbols, the poetic symbols, of life."

Something of the same spirit informs late Doris Lessing, late Clarice

Pablo Picasso, *Self Portrait Facing Death* (1972)

Lispector. It informs late Titian; late Rembrandt, with those heavy, often haphazard looking brushstrokes; those late cut-outs by Matisse; the raw cartoony cigar-chomping Klansmen of Guston. It's everywhere in Dylan of course—not just the Sinatra songs and Christmas tunes. It's there in late Coltrane, late Tom Waits, late Leonard Cohen, late Beatles, late Angela Carter . . . all those scruffy, late blooming flowers going rogue from the garden, in search of rougher ground. "The maturity of late works," Said writes, paraphrasing Adorno, "does not resemble the kind one finds in fruit. They are . . . not round, but furrowed, even ravaged . . . bitter and spiny, they do not surrender themselves to mere delectation."

Leonard Michaels, like his better-known contemporary Roth, evolved a distinct new style in his late work, the unfinished cycle known as the Nachman Stories. Here, too, the movement of maturity is less a matter of contraction than expansion. Michaels launched himself into literary space with a prose of aggressive, propulsive force, a rebel in flight from immigrant parents and obscure species guilts. The tense, leathery diction of the early prose—("I didn't budge. I stared. His eyes squeezed to dashes. I heard the mock whimper of yawns. He began scratching the tablecloth.")—was its hallmark feature. But with time and wear the fabric of that prose begins to soften, bagging out at the joints like an old coat, mellowing into a kind of quizzical vulnerability, revealing the emotional and epistemological confusions of a mathematician for whom the workings of the world remain a strange, insoluble equation.

> He yearned for his office and his desk and the window that looked out on the shining Pacific. He'd never gone swimming in the prodigious, restless, teeming, alluring thing, but he loved the changing light on its surface and the sounds it made in the darkness. . . . A man began playing a guitar. The tune was a bossa nova, haunting, something like a blues, only more finely nuanced and not at all macho. . . . Soon he wasn't thinking at all, only following the tune. It made a lovely, sinuous shape, and then made it again and again, always a little differently and yet always the same, as the rhythm carried its exquisite sadness toward infinity.

It's like the return of a prodigal son. The bad boy has grown up; has shed his calcified, knowing postures and attitudes, and embraced his inner schlemiel. What a transformation! He no longer sounds like a hard-nosed Isaac Babel; he sounds more like some bewildered, dreamy refugee from Malamud or Chekhov, a new arrival in a strange land. And isn't that the hope of us all, that as we go on living and working over the course of a long life, the point of our departure and the point of our arrival might curve under the weight of the ultimate necessity, and at last converge? After all, the meter of mortality is ticking; whither should we bend our steps? Who knows what work we might be capable of if, like the Grandmother in Flannery O'Connor's story, there was someone there to shoot us every minute of our lives?

These are of course rhetorical questions. For a rhetorical answer, or the ghost of one, I'd like to conclude with a writer whose own style—in its eerie plainness, its dogged devotion to paradox, its refusal of lyric consolation, its lack of interest in any unifying theory or stance or proclamation— seems so consistently and mysteriously "late" as to approach the posthumous.

> "Every limb as tired as a person."
> "Let the bad remain bad, otherwise it will grow worse."
> "Does my larynx hurt so much because for many hours I have done nothing with it?"
> "So the help goes away again without helping."

These are literally the last words Kafka ever wrote. They're taken from the brief notes, or "conversation slips," he'd jot down to his nurses, friends, and doctors in the Kierling sanatorium as he lay dying of tuberculosis. No other form of communication was possible; his larynx had shut like a door. Aptly enough, he was proofreading the galleys of "A Hunger Artist" at the time, that painstaking fable of a self closing down, doing without. And yet for all his suffering and deprivation there is no bitterness or rage to be found in these notes, only his usual modest and immaculate courtesy, and maybe a somewhat keener than usual observance of (and doting regard for) the struggles of the various life forms around him, increasingly precious as they recede from view. Is there a line in his stories more poignant than the note he writes, in his last days, after a glass he's knocked over shatters on the floor: "You'll have to warn the girl about the glass; she sometimes comes in barefoot?" Did he—did *any*one—ever write anything more raw and more refined, more fancy and more plain, more simple and more complex, more true to the ecstasies of life in all its sentience, beauty, and appetite, than this glimpse at the flowers dying on the windowsill beside him:

"How wonderful that is, isn't it? The lilac—dying, it drinks, goes on swilling."

Refer Madness

Writing in an Age of Allusion

❧

Here in its entirety is a short story by Kafka, called "The Wish to be a Red Indian":

> If one were only an Indian, instantly alert, and on a racing horse, leaning against the wind, kept on quivering jerkily over the quivering ground, until one shed one's spurs, for there needed no spurs, threw away the reins, for there needed no reins, and hardly saw that the land before one was smoothly shorn heath when horse's neck and head would be already gone.

This sentence, a plaintive and mysterious journey into white space, both expresses and embodies a yearning as physical as it is metaphysical, a yearning typical of its writer and indeed all writers: the wish to be a more natural, less self-conscious being. Or to put it another way, to not be a writer at all. Let's face it, no one's better at writing about not wanting to be a writer than someone who actually *is* a writer. And among writers, no one's better than Kafka, for whom wanting and being are almost never in synch. "The impossibility of not writing, the impossibility of writing German, the impossibility of writing differently," he laments in a letter. "One might also add a fourth impossibility, the impossibility of writing."

He's hardly alone in this. "Live, live all you can," Henry James, the Master himself says, or rather writes, "it's a mistake not to." Only living is not quite James's thing—or Kafka's either. Why not trade in all that brooding, all that irritability and eye strain, for the life of an (okay, absurdly caricatured and fake-mythic) "Indian"? Who doesn't want to be wild and natural and sure, to plunge head-long through space with such velocity and purpose that no spurs or reins are necessary? Though head-*short* would be more accurate, for the head in Kafka's story, when it finally appears, is already something of an afterthought, syntactically and existentially attenuated . . . a head, the story concludes, "already gone."

We find this same itch for unfettered animal movement—for an existence reduced, or maybe enhanced, to mere body-in-motion, shorn of mental entanglements and obligations and "quivering with the fever of life"—everywhere in Kafka's work, to say nothing of his life. Take this entry in the *Octavo Notebooks*: "He leaves the house, he finds himself in the street, a horse is waiting, a servant is holding the stirrup, the ride takes him through an echoing wilderness." Or the narrator of "The Departure," who having ordered his servant to fetch his horse from the stables, is stopped at the gate and asked where he's going. "I don't know," he says, "just out of here, just out of here. Out of here, nothing else, it's the only way I can reach my goal." "So you know your goal?" the servant asks. "Yes," he replies, "I've just told you. Out of here—that's my goal."

But of course you can't *get* out of here in Kafka's world. There may be horses, but they are never ours; there may be Indians, but they are never us; there may be gates that lend access to the Law, but they're forever closed. *Always hope, but not for us.* For us there are only shackles, cages, constrictions. We are not pure beings, not whole selves, not animals, not gods. For all the purity of our aspirations we live, as Kafka did, in a compromised space, in rooms sandwiched by other rooms, selves hemmed in by other selves. Trapped between two realms, the earthly and the heavenly, we're unable to fully inhabit or escape either one. We can only gesture longingly in both directions, flailing our useless limbs, like an upended dung beetle trying to get out of bed.

"It's the old joke," Kafka writes. "We hold the world fast and complain that it is holding us."

Which brings me to my subject: our ways of holding the world fast, even in fiction—*especially* in fiction—and how the faster the great world spins, the tighter we clutch onto its fabric. And I mean this literally. I mean with our fingers. With those busy, groping digital instruments we call our hands.

Speaking of digital instruments, it's been pretty well documented by now that this great web we're all caught in and borne up by is changing us in fundamental ways, affecting not just how we interact (or don't), but how we read (ditto) and think (ditto). And how do I know this? The same way you do. By power-browsing websites, skimming articles by the likes of Nicholas Carr and Jaron Lanier (or rather skimming articles by *other* writers who have skimmed articles by the likes of Carr and Lanier) memorizing a fact or two, a quote or two, and interweaving it with my own anecdotal experience and those of friends. This is what passes for "knowledge" these days. There's no need to make a moral judgment about this—or maybe there *is* a need, a really pressing need actually, but not by me—but it's worth pondering the implications for both writers and readers.

Where reading is concerned we all know the liturgy by now, and can recite it by heart like our own gloomy Spenglerian *Kol Nidre. Our Father Our King, we have sinned before you: we've scanned, we've skimmed, we've clicked on stuff we shouldn't have clicked on, we've skipped blithely from link to link for hours at a time and retained nothing; and in some not entirely coincidental way the prospect of starting, let alone finishing, the sort of fat three-decker novels we used to devour almost routinely*—Middlemarch, The Magic Mountain, The Man Who Loved Children—*has become as lonely and remote, as haloed by a nimbus of virtuous nostalgia, as a trip to the moon.*

It's not our fault by the way. We weren't born like this. "We are not only what we read, we are *how* we read," the developmental psychologist Maryanne Wolf informs us. Reading is not an instinctual behavior but a learned one: doing it repeatedly over time rewires the neural circuits in our brains. (Readers of ideograms, for example, develop different mental pathways than those dependent upon an alphabet.) Given that the average American spends eight hours a day in front of a screen, that's a lot of rewiring going on. No wonder our heads feel so thronged. We're like people who spend too much time in the gym: for all our furious efforts somehow at the end of the day (and the day, these days, never does seem to end) we haven't actually *gone* anywhere. Meanwhile the data keeps coming, the screens keep flaring with numbers and light.

"When things come at you very fast," warned Marshall McLuhan, decades before the Internet, "naturally you lose touch with yourself." Around the same time, his fellow Canadian Saul Bellow echoed a similar concern: "If there is no significant space, there is no judgment, no freedom, we determine nothing for ourselves *individually* . . . it leaves us helplessly in the public sphere. Then to say that the world is too much with us is meaningless for there is no longer any us. The world is *everything*."

If there is no longer any us, only world, where does that leave the inner life? If our reading is changing, then our thinking must be changing. And if our thinking is changing, then so inevitably is both how and what we write. And if things are coming at us faster and faster, and the private self is besieged, where will we find the time and space necessary to read a novel, let alone write one?

As long as a century ago Walter Benjamin spoke of a menacing increase in information, "incompatible with the spirit of story-telling. . . . A rustling in the leaves that drives away . . . the dream-bird that hatches the egg of experience." And when the same machine one writes and often reads one's dreamy stories upon also happens to be a roaring leaf-blower in its own right? When technology has invaded the very means by which we try to escape it? No wonder it's so hard to get any fucking work done.

But perhaps this was always the case. "Our writing equipment," Nietzsche wrote in 1881, "takes part in the forming of our thoughts." And he should know. Once he switched from pen to typewriter, his own prose rhythms, never exactly temperate to begin with, turned up to eleven. Those staccato aphorisms, terrible puns, and emphatic proclamations pummeling the page like a machine—what were they if not the brutal clattering of a new technology seeking expression?

Writers of my own generation, we who wrote our first books on hulking IBM Selectrics, understand this all too well. Those days when you'd have no words in your head and yet go on typing anyway, borne along by that furious, thrummingly electrical current. But then along came the nineties, and the giddy liberation of "word processing." To be relieved of all that laborious retyping! That tedious and interminable cutting and pasting! And yet after a while, once the novelty was gone, the suspicion began to dawn that maybe the great liberator was in fact only another occupier, another ruthless autocrat laying down his own silent but insidious laws. If the bars of the cell are made of plastic, not iron, does that make them any less confining?

Whether it makes them *more* confining is a question well worth asking, or Googling, or typing into one's smartphone, provided of course one *has* a smartphone, which I, for one, didn't use to. I held out against smartphones for years. I was perfectly content with my own phone, which was in retrospect very dumb indeed, a phone so slab-like and lethargic, so not-gifted and not-talented, so remedial and inexpressive, it could barely get it up to ring. My phone had no clue what an app was. It sent no email, it played no music, it had no GPS, and if I held it up to one of those little squares of frozen static that sit like Rorschach blots beside every material item in every shop in America, my phone just stared at it uncomprehendingly, breathing through whatever the equivalent of its mouth was. To be fair, at some point my phone was the very newest, smartest thing, sleek and powerful as a phaser. But I didn't buy it at that point. No, by the point I bought it, the heyday of your basic Samsung clamshell flip-style had long since passed into history—like the rotary dial, the telegraph, and the carrier pigeon before it—which was why I was able to get it so cheap (the only thing I cared about) and why when I brought it home my children snickered at this latest evidentiary exhibit in that losing trial, my life.

But never mind. I hesitated to buy a smartphone for a very simple reason: because I knew I would abuse it. Like most people who cultivate an air of brooding intensity, I am in fact a rather shallow person with lousy concentration and dilettante-ish tendencies. Already I do not so much live my life as *refer* to it. Each day presents another Talmudic text to be glossed and parsed, a dense, ever-evolving set of symbolic narratives that can only be comprehended, or for that matter endured, by a lot of brain-numbing intertextual commentary. Nothing is ever simply itself. No thought is ever solo or unencumbered. Everything arrives with an entourage of associations, a posse of references that loiter in my head, emptying the mini-bar and stealing the robes. Every raging old man reminds me of Lear; every big talker seems straight out of Bellow; every unhappy family Tolstoyan in its own way. The sleepy look Oblomovian; the restless and nomadic Chatwinian; the hungry Hamsunian; the melancholy and bored Chekhovian; and the sight of my enormous honker in the mirror, it goes without saying, forever and absurdly Gogolesque. In short, there is no element of my conscious life (about my unconscious life I can't say; I am unconscious of my unconscious life) free of referentiality, and this was true before I even *owned* a smartphone.

My wife for one finds this referencing tendency objectionable, not just on the obvious grounds (i.e., that it makes me tiresome and pedantic, like a clerk in a used bookstore) but on a deeper, more spiritual level as well. That is, if I am always busy comparing and referring things to other things, then I am never just *being*. And the person I am never just being, in her view, is myself. No wonder I hate yoga and meditation, she thinks. No wonder I won't sign up for mindfulness retreats, or go hiking, or sit still for five minutes without opening a book or a magazine and having at least two different media outlets making noise in the background. My head, in her view, is a too-open book. Everything that goes on inside has a set of corresponding, infinitely more pressing references outside, and everything outside has a set of corresponding, infinitely more pressing references inside, and so most of the time my life is neither here nor there but rather, as Milan Kundera might say, elsewhere.

Case in point: in an ideal world I would not have made reference to Milan Kundera just now, because it sounds so blatantly pretentious. Especially as I'm only name-checking the *title* of one of his (best, in my opinion) novels, as opposed to the substance. Then too ideally I would not go on to compare this condition I'm describing—of feeling like one slender but heavily annotated volume in a vast universal library—to the work of Borges or Carl Jung, though in truth these *do* seem fair if not inevitable comparisons. But there you are: there appears to be no way to diagnose this particular affliction that doesn't also succumb to it. No matter how you struggle to wriggle free from the headlock of referentiality, there's no way out, only further in, submitting to its muscular, protean grip, forever ransacking the mind's library for references to others who have in wrestling with this same tendency made reference to still others, everyone flopping and thrashing in the same capacious, infinitely pliable net.

Well, you're thinking, *so what*? It's the postmodern condition. Our heads are lit up like switchboards with secondhand data, viral videos, forwarded articles and listicles, twitters and tweets. Nothing to be done. Anyway it's not such a terrible affliction in the scheme of things, walking around with a library vaster than Alexandria's bulging in your pants. That access to knowledge, or information anyway, is no longer the preserve of the elitely educated, seems like a positive development for instance. And if the cost of that access is a brave new world where everyone is constantly looking shit up on their phones, and every haphazard opinion at a dinner party gets fact-checked and shot down by some wise guy Googling under the table, and every movie comes annotated with a hailstorm of factoids from the IMDB (not just the gross receipts but the AD, the filmography of the script supervisor, and the name of the catering company that supplied the bagels), and an unsettling suspicion, as you flit from link to link, that someone's making *money* from the crumbs of data you're leaving behind, that what seems like voluntary behavior is in fact the result of manipulation and design, that it's maybe a little harder than it used to be to concentrate on, well, *any*thing, to locate, amidst so much refracted noise, the attenuated beam of your own personal signal . . . well, so be it. Every revolution, as they say, has its winners and losers.

Besides, notions of the "personal" and the "original," absent the usual ironic air quotes, haven't aged very well. They're faded and baggy these days, like old tee-shirts: you can hardly go out in them anymore. *Irony* itself, of course, will never go out of style. It wobbled a little at the turn of the century, but it's come back strong on social media, which rewards clever glosses and cool takes of all kinds. That it's a soul-destroying enterprise that blurs the line between glibness and intelligence, that preys rapaciously upon resources it cheapens and diminishes along the way, is unfortunate, but what can you do? That's just life under, you know, *Late Capitalism*.

Anyway what's so great about originality? The energies of evolution, in art and in life, are braided, interconnecting, codependent; we progress—*if* we progress—not by leaps and bounds but by tiny incremental variations. Nothing goes away. Everything gets recycled. Nature does not know extinction, all it knows is transformation. I stole that line from

Thomas Pynchon by the way, who, in turn, took it from Werner von Braun. And God knows where *he* got it. Does it matter?

Pynchon himself has never shied away from name-checking his influences. Like *V*'s Herbert Stencil, he likes to strew discrete bits of referential data around the page like clues at a crime scene, making us do the detective work of connecting the dots. All the while there's the suspicion that the joke may be on *us*: that no one dunnit. That no one stands behind the curtain, working the levers; that confronted with the mysterious case that is the world, we can't help weaving little paranoid conspiracies out of whole cloth; that we prefer an imagined coherence, even a fabricated one, over no coherence at all. None of which is an original insight, really. Doubtless Pynchon got it from previous books, like William Gaddis's *The Recognitions* (a novel all about the virtues and/or necessities of copying Old Masters), which includes this droll little shorthand, hidden in the foliage of that massive text: "*Orignlty not inventn bt snse of recall, recgntion, pattrns alrdy thr.*"

Viewed half a century later, from the far side of the postmodern age, this notion of originality as discovery rather than invention seems so obvious, so ubiquitous—so *unoriginal* really—that it's almost too boring to talk about. "I wonder if this thing we call originality," David Mitchell says in an interview, "isn't an electric motor powered by the two poles off the already done and the new twist, or the familiar and the far-out." If that sounds a bit mechanistic, Mitchell feels no need to apologize: like Pynchon, or his more obvious influence, Murakami, he likes to conflate high and low forms in his work, as happy to plunder from Captain Jack Sparrow or *The Matrix* as from Nabokov, Borges, and Calvino. This can get a bit wearing. Reading *Cloud Atlas*, for example, with its zigzagging narratives, its gorgeously over-stuffed set-pieces and its declamatory rhetorical flourishes, is like being locked in the wardrobe closet of some insanely well-funded provincial theater company. Let's see, what have we here? A sea captain's hat, a tweedy English jacket, a pair of leather pants from San Francisco, a florid silken waistcoat in the Ottoman style, some sort of fusiony, futuristic kimono . . . what happens if we, oh I don't know, throw them all together? The conflation of so many disparate narrative vocabularies in a single work (sea story, dystopian sci-fi, seventies political thriller, etc.) creates its own dizzying but also sometimes enervating, centrifugal effects. But Mitchell doesn't mind. He's content to go by Samuel Goldwyn's brazen, cheerful maxim: "Let's have some new clichés."

Despite if not because of this, he strikes me as a representative writer for the globalized age, in that he makes our enormous, trembling web of referential interconnectivity both subject and method, engine and fuel. To him it's a *good* thing. For all the violence and melodrama in his work he offers an affirmative vision, the bright side of the Pynchonian moon. (Gaddis again: "Separateness, that's what went wrong. . . . Everything withholding itself from everything else. . . . Everything vain, asserting itself"). His characters move like clouds across spatial and temporal lines, drifting along preexistent song-lines towards memory and myth, towards deeply inlaid species codes. The coherence he projects is fatalistic but not gloomy, an arc of history that bends inevitably towards justice. Here we are, he seems to say, still sitting by the same old fires, telling the same old stories, in the same old tent cities . . . isn't that great? "Old and new make the warp and woof of every moment," Emerson writes. "There is no thread that is not a twist of these two strands. By necessity, by proclivity, and by delight, we all quote."

Of course upon closer examination, every strand of the old is revealed to be a double or triple helix in its own right, as I have just demonstrated for example by quoting Emerson in a way that implies I have a volume of his essays open beside me, when in truth I took the words not from Emerson himself, but from Jonathan Lethem's ingenious *Harpers* piece, "The Ecstasy of Influence"—an essay that manages to document, investigate, and (because it's comprised entirely of quotes) formally embody the "open source" view of art at the same. And I suspect that Lethem, as he wrote, didn't have Emerson's essays open on *his* desk either.

It's all fair use, in other words—in fact in *those* words—and that's fine. Same as it ever was. After all plagiarism, as plagiarists are forever eager to remind us, is strictly a modern concept. The ancient poets copied freely, often verbatim and without citation, recasting earlier works to suit their own purposes and tastes. The Hebrews rip off the Canaanites. Virgil rips off Homer, who wasn't even Homer. Dante rips off Virgil. Matthew and Luke rip off Mark. Shakespeare rips off Plutarch, Eliot rips off Shakespeare, Dylan rips off everyone, and George Harrison, of all people, rips off the Chiffons. And so it goes. Literary influence is a long-running, ever-expanding business, endlessly profitable and self-renewing. Or to put it in less romantic terms: *Language is the common whore whom each writer tries to make his own bitch.*

That's a direct verbatim quote from Auden by the way, though it pains me to cite him in this context, as I haven't *read* Auden in years, and consequently have no idea how and where I came by this quote—which is therefore come to think of it not direct at all, and maybe not verbatim either. Maybe it's not even Auden. It sounds, honestly, more like Mickey Spillane. If I stopped writing this essay and took out my smartphone I could tell you for sure. Though no doubt by now you've taken out your own smartphones, and can just as easily tell *me*.

In any case, whatever you want to call this tradition (fair use, open source, public commons, digital sampling), the question it poses for the working artist and that other beleaguered species, the individual in society, is whether it expands into a world of exhilarating possibilities, or flattens down everything into one shallow, nauseating plane of the already-done.

I'm thinking of someone like John Leonard, the late, much esteemed book critic, who liked to review major novels in the manner of a coked-up host at some bold-faced cocktail party. Just for laughs, scan his *NY Times* review of *Harry Potter and the Order of the Phoenix* sometime. First the early arrivals, Tolkien, Joseph Campbell, and C. S. Lewis, come trooping down the foyer; then you proceed, by way of Wonderland, Camelot, Brigadoon, Macondo, and Oz, into the library, where William Blake, George Orwell, Jacques Lacan, Lewis Carroll, Cyrus of Herodotus, St. John of the Cross, St. Teresa of Avila, the Old Testament, the New Testament, the Hindu Krishna, the Epic of Gilgamesh, and the Song of Roland await. Along the way you'll stop to greet some boisterous, colorfully-dressed old friends: Mary Poppins, the Brothers Grimm, Scheherazade, Hercules, Godzilla, Sinbad the Sailor, the Flying Dutchman, Luke Skywalker, T. H. White, *Snow* White, Peter Pan, Caliban, Superman, and Doctor Who. And wait, did you forget Judith Krantz? Because you can be sure Leonard didn't. How could you forget Judith freaking Krantz?

However easy it is to make fun of Leonard's promiscuous way with the caps key, he's hardly unique in this department. The entire oeuvre of George Steiner reads, as John Simon once said, "like a university library card catalogue hit by a tornado." This is more or less what critics *do* with books: fling other books against them like spaghetti against a wall, and then see what sticks.

Never mind that the bulk of such references are, as any honest writer will concede, accidental. It's the reader who gets the final say. "Intertextuality," writes the theorist Don Fowler, "like all aspects of literary reception, is ultimately located in reading practice. Meaning is realized at the point of reception." The very form of criticism like Steiner's and Leonard's reminds us that connectivity is how the novel thrives: that no work is truly singular, but demands to be read in the constelled lights of other work, lights it both absorbs and then atomizes in every direction—

towards works already written and those far off in the dark matter, waiting to emerge.

Borges, in his short essay "Kafka and His Precursors," takes this idea, as he takes everything, one step further in the direction of the cosmic. "The fact is that each writer creates his precursors. His work modifies our conception of the past, as it will modify the future. In this correlation, the identity or plurality of men doesn't matter." The essay unfurls for us a multidimensional map of literary influence where the streets are neither one-way nor two-way, but an infinite series of forking paths. Like Gaddis and Mitchell, Borges, the great librarian, seeks at once to undermine our notions of originality and to rescue them from laziness and convention by directing us into the labyrinth of the stacks, forcing us to work our way through.

Let's pause here to concede the obvious: novels have *always* depended upon reference, both intertextual to previous novels and extratextual, to the great, teeming world beyond. Think of Stendhal's Paris, Dickens's (or Zadie Smith's) London, Joyce's Dublin, Paley's New York, Lispector's Rio, Shafak's Istanbul, Babel's Odessa, Hrabal's Prague, Roth's Newark, Didion's L. A., Bellow's Chicago. All of these settings are fictional, but none are invented. Or is it the other way around? God knows the pages of these books are dense with recognizable place names and thoroughfares, their atmospheres sooty with particles of the real, the preexisting, the unalterable, the uninventable. It's true that some novels go almost too far in this direction, exhibit such servile deferentiality to the real as to approach the fetishistic. But the best of them weave a web of illusion and allusion that can't be untangled.

"I hate things all fiction," Byron wrote. "There should always be some foundation of fact for the most airy fabric—and pure invention is but the talent of a liar."

Consider that quaint nineteenth-century convention, the name dash (as in "That day she made the long train journey to S—"), which conflates realism and artifice in such a way as to make the whole distinction irrelevant. It suggests at once the authority of personal discretion (you and I both know who or what I'm really talking about here, so why spell it out?) and the impersonal mystery of art (why *not* spell it out?). That's a genuine achievement. It blurs the line between what goes on inside the margins and what goes on outside, makes it porous, ambiguous, a subject of narrative wonder and tension. Countless writers of what's now arguably too often referred to as "autofiction"—Kenzaburo Oe, Marguerite Duras, Karl Ove Knausgaard, Ben Lerner, Sheila Heti, Rachel Cusk, Jean Rhys, and so on—have explored this blurred seam to great effect, delineating a topography of self with such a receptive, finely-tuned antenna it almost, but not quite, vanishes up the writer's lower intestines.

Not that this was the sort of fact-foundation Byron had in mind. Nor, in all likelihood, would he have approved of fictions like Kafka's or Beckett's, which are almost mystically *purged* of fact, shorn of any recognizable foundation other than the grave. And yet writers on the other, more material end of the spectrum, who litter their work with the proper nouns of the day, probably wouldn't charm him all that much either.

How much narrative purity, in short, do we need or want? How much of our reading of *Don Quixote*, say, or *Madame Bovary*, depends upon an acquaintance with the popular romances of their respective eras? How to absorb the work of radical modernists like Virginia Woolf, if not in light of the very pre-modern conventions they're rejecting? High-modern works of systemic parody, like *Ulysses* and *Lolita*, depend on our willingness to make reference to bodies of extratextual material. And then postmodernism comes along to gleefully ride that horse into the sunset.

Or *towards* the sunset, anyway. Somehow with postmodernism we never do quite make it to the terminal point, but invariably wind up stranded in that noisy, brightly-lit cul-de-sac we call pastiche. Pastiche gets a bad rap these days ("parody without any of parody's ulterior motives," Frederic Jameson calls it, "amputated of the satiric impulse, devoid of laughter") in the same way Las Vegas gets a bad rap. And yet both have their appeal, their little pleasures, and maybe a certain cultural inevitability too. "Ironically," Kurt Anderson remarks,

> new technology has reinforced the nostalgic cultural gaze: now that we have instant universal access to every old image and recorded sound, the future has arrived and it's all about dreaming of the past. Our culture's primary M.O. now consists of promiscuously and sometimes compulsively reviving and rejiggering old forms. It's the rare "new" cultural artifact that doesn't seem a lot like a cover version of something we've seen or heard before. Which means the very idea of datedness has lost the power it possessed during most of our lifetimes.

Even as we decry the loss of the original, and grow weary of cannibalizing the museum, we can't help relishing the opportunities for playful fucking around—for trying on masks and appropriating genres—that are increasingly available to us. "Writers signify upon each other's texts," writes Henry Louis Gates, "by rewriting the received textual tradition." We're so accustomed to this signifying by now, absorbed so much of it in music, film, painting, and photography, we're no longer even conscious of it as such. Sometimes it seems like *everything* is referentiality and pastiche. That nothing in our culture is immune to those viral, corrosive germs. These are the moments that make us almost literally sick. Because whatever else you want to say about it, whatever aesthetic justifications you want to advance, there are times when it all begins to seem like so much smart-alecky, liberal-artsy dick-swinging: a low-impact sport where the brainiacs and bookworms finally get picked first.

Still, sometimes it's nice just to be on a team.

Anyway, like it or not, Benjamin was right: there's no going back. The tide of information isn't likely to recede anytime soon. We have to find a way not to drown in it. And to register those things that might indeed drown, before they do. "Literature cannot compete with wonderful technology," Bellow writes. "But isn't there a branch of the wonderful into which wonderful technology cannot lead us?"

We have to hope so. Our Grand Allusions should serve not as destinations, but departure points. Not discoveries, but "recogntns." Whatever forms that will take are impossible to predict in anything but their multiplicity, their instability, their spirit of "impure invention." Neither the lie of pure originality, nor the echo chamber of mere secondhand reference, will do. "Nothing more original, nothing more unique than to feed off others," Valery writes. "But they must be digested—*the lion achieves his form by assimilating sheep.*"

Which reminds me of one final point of reference: to a writer I mentioned earlier, Rachel Cusk. In *Outline* we have a novel which rather remarkably conforms to Valery's idea, a novel which, like the narrator herself, appears to feed entirely off of others, achieving its own form—an outline of its own—in the process of assimilation.

> He was describing, she realized, a distinction that seemed to grow clearer and clearer the more he talked, a distinction he stood on one side of while she, it became increasingly apparent, stood on the other. He was describing, in other words, what she herself was not: in everything he said about himself, she found in her own nature a corresponding negative. This anti-description, for want of a better way of putting it, had made something clear to her by a reverse kind of exposition: while he talked she began to see herself as a shape, an

outline, with all the detail filled in around it while the shape itself remained blank. Yet this shape, even while its content remained unknown, gave her for the first time since the incident a sense of who she now was.

All of which takes us a long way from Kafka's Red Indian, that pure, untrammeled being. Or does it? Maybe in the end Kafka is too austere, too much the perfectionist control-freak, too averse to the contaminations and compromises around him, in art and in life, to go on. Because none of us, in the end, *are* Red Indians. We're more like the mouse folk who listen to Josephine, or the crowd that files by the Hunger Artist's cage—transfixed, for a while anyway, by our admiration for that very purity we can neither achieve nor maintain, before our return to the stream of human traffic he calls the *Verkeh.*

But here's the thing: even Kafka's brief story is not entirely pure or reference-free. It too directs our attention out from the text—first to whatever a "Red Indian" might be, and then to a larger historical context that might help us comprehend why a finicky, neurotic German-centric Jew in the middle of the Austro-Hungarian empire might invoke that particular reference. If ours is not an age of pure expression, neither was Kafka's. *No* age is particularly conducive to purity; doubtless that's why we're forever longing for it. (Didn't minimalism flourish in the 1960s?) So fine. Even if it's true that accelerated access to data will continue to tip the balance of contemporary literature even further from invention to fact; even if it's true that much of what results will be heavily-Googled works of "realism" that depend upon the very technology they're attacking to provide the weapons they will use, feebly for the most part, against it; even if it's true that the rubber bands of reference can stretch only so far before they snap—we're still impelled onward by the same old atavistic urgings to communicate. Still using language like feelers, inching our way towards the edge beyond which language can't go: the happiness (as they say) that writes white.

Living, Loving, Temple-Going

Men resist the conclusion in the morning, but adopt it as the evening wears on, that temper prevails over everything of time, place, and condition, and is inconsumable in the flames of religion.

—Emerson, "Experience"

I. Jewboy's Complaint

In 1981 I moved from San Francisco to New York with the idea of turning myself into a writer. I was twenty-four. I had no job, no money, no prospects, not much in the way of talent, and, it seemed increasingly clear, only the flimsiest and most attenuated sense of an identity. No flag to plant, and nowhere to plant it. Turning myself into a writer, as things turned out, wasn't even the hard part; the hard part was turning myself into a *self*. I had come to New York in the throes of a ruinous love affair, one that seemed to rob me not just of my hopes for the future but all sense of a coherent past as well. Any ongoing continuity between the person I'd thought myself to be and the smaller, less adequate person who went by the same name had vanished. Who was this guy? A field of negative spaces. A net full of holes. A person not quite young, not quite grown up, not quite Jewish, not quite a student, not quite a worker, not quite a person really. The only thing I appeared to be good for—good at—was reading novels. Novels were what moved me. They moved me much more powerfully, sad to say, than that dubious and provisional sphere people called the real world.

Meanwhile my now ex-girlfriend from the Bay Area—with whom I'd painstakingly planned this move to New York—had flown to Israel, where she proceeded to marry some other, presumably better person entirely. It's important to mention, and boy did she mention it, that she'd been born in Israel. Her parents were Auschwitz survivors who'd met in a DP camp, emigrated to Palestine and settled on a kibbutz. Her beloved father loved it there, her quarrelsome mother not so much. At some point the latter decamped to San Francisco, and the former—a fervent Zionist—followed her, only to subsequently die young, whether of cancer or heartbreak or both. To say my ex nurtured a historical grudge against the diaspora would

74

be an understatement. To her a Jew's life in this moronic inferno was irrelevant at best; at worst it was neither Jewish nor life at all. Under her scrutiny the bloated, cheerfully benign surface of American culture looked like a killing field, a weightless and colorless final solution in which all higher purposes and traditions dissolved into nothing. The pop pleasures it offered, though enjoyable, were neither serious nor sustaining. No, America wasn't for her: that much was clear. This was one desert she had no patience to see bloom.

All of which she'd undertaken to explain to me the first time we met. Also the last time we met. Also a number of times between.

For the most part I kept quiet. Such was my self-absorption, I was only half-listening to what she was saying; the other half was excited by how hotly and ferociously she was saying it, the furious blaze of her convictions, her contempts. Here at last was that formidable Other, the one I'd been waiting all my life to fall in love with. And how did I know this? Because she appeared to have no use for me at all. Why should she? I was too young, too inexperienced, too smug, too casual; most of what I knew was from books. In fact much of our affair was conducted in the shadow of a new Philip Roth novel I happened to be reading at the time, *The Ghost Writer*—a book about an assimilated young man with literary pretensions who falls in love with a gaunt, soulful, and elusive beauty who might well be Anne Frank, who seems to carry the dead of Europe around in the black bags under her eyes. This was a little unfortunate, at least for her, as no one likes to be confused with a character in a novel, absorbed into someone else's imaginative hero's journey from innocence to experience. But my ex was far too spikey and mercurial in the flesh, too full of sweeping and intemperate opinions—too real, in short—to submit to a mere literary conceit. Don't get *her* started on the Philip Roths of the world. Don't try to charm *her* with that tired nostalgia act, Jewish-American culture. All those Bellows and Berles and Bennys and Bruces, those Ginsbergs and Dylans and Leonard Cohens . . . what did they know about Jewish anger, Jewish tragedy, Jewish need? She gazed down on their tiresome antics the same way Naomi, Roth's poster-child sabra, gazed down on Portnoy's: as the impotent flailing of the diaspora neurotic, who knows neither who he is nor what he wants.

It was a pretty persuasive argument, I thought. Nonetheless I had my own history, and that of the Enlightenment, whispering in my ear the whole time, calling into question this poster-child Zionism of hers. Wasn't it a little backwards and regressive, politically speaking—a retreat into nationalism and its discontents? Hadn't those wars been won? Hadn't we

75

all moved on to universal humanism or something? I was ready to concede that American–Jewish culture had its shortcomings, but what culture didn't? Weren't its fruits, all those tasty Grouchos and Rothkos, as nourishing and legitimate as any others, if not just possibly (I couldn't help thinking) a little more so? I too was something of a poster child, damn it: the Diaspora's favorite son. A suburban Reform kid, New Jersey division. Okay maybe we weren't paratroopers or intelligence officers. Maybe the only battle sounds we heard were the thundrous roar of lawn mowers on a summer afternoon. Maybe all we retained from our traditions was an attenuated, vaguely sentimental tribalism, vestigial but tenacious, like a phantom limb. Was it our fault if we regarded the Chosen People less as a holy cause than a beloved but embattled small-market sports franchise, a team whose fortunes, for all the media attention they generated, were forever suspended precipitously over an abyss? Why did my parents root so vociferously for Tom Okker, a diminutive Dutch tennis player who regularly lost in the quarter-finals, anyway? Because he was *Jewish!* Why did they love Tony Curtis? Because *Bernie Schwartz!* Kirk Douglas? *Issur Demsky!* Lauren Bacall? *Bette Joan Perske!* Our life was a long-running, seemingly uncancellable quiz show called Name That Jew. Every question you asked led to the same answer. Alan King? *Jewish!* Norman Mailer? *Jewish!* Baskin? *Jewish!* Robbins? *Jewish!* Sammy Davis Jr.? *Jewish!* Paul Newman? Okay, *half*-Jewish, to be precise, but half was better than nothing. A *lot* better.

Point being, when it came to continuity with the tribe, we made do with what we had. And we didn't have all that much, frankly. We were two generations removed from a coherent communal identity, from the bonds and bondedness of the mitzvot. Sunday school was a joke, Hebrew school a *bad* joke. And let's not go into the bar mitzvahs. Let's not talk about the *onegs*, the sponge cakes, the little thimbles of Manischewitz that left bloody rings on the white tablecloths. Let's leave aside that after a dozen years of "study," my comprehension of Judaic law amounted to a lamentable pastiche, a crazy-quilt of random exhortations—*Never Again! Next Year in Jerusalem! Sandy Koufax Didn't Pitch on Yom Kippur! Bob Dylan Sends His Kids to Jewish camps!*—along with a tentative conviction that somewhere in the coiled scrolls of the Torah there was a law that mandated, a couple of days every autumn, the suspension of alternate-side-of-the-street parking.

No, it wasn't much. For all my Jewish airs I was flying, or floating rather, on threadbare wings. A *luftmensch* more *luft* than *mensch*. True, I had the historical *shnoz*; the ironical, self-deprecating temperament; the long sloping *punim* in which could be plainly seen, as I was often reminded, the entire map of Poland. True, if a Jew, as Sartre said, is someone others take as a Jew, then arguably everything I did, however ignorant and secularized, was essentially Jewish. I would have liked to believe that was the case. In fact I was pretty sure my rabbi had said something along those lines in Hebrew School, on those rare occasions he wasn't warning, in sepulchral tones, of the dangers of intermarriage, which would plunge the final dagger into the heart of that tremulous outpatient, the Jewish people.

"*As a little bit of musk fills an entire house,*" wrote Osip Mandelstam, "*so the least influence of Judaism overflows all of one's life.*"

It's a good line. Who knows, maybe if I'd used it on my ex, she'd have stuck around smelling the musk a while longer. But probably not. Mandelstam, Shmandelstam: believe me, it would have taken more than poetry to pry that El Al ticket from her fist, that lifelong shadow of Oedipal destiny from her heart. In the end, it seemed, there really *were* distinctions to be made between one kind of Jew and another kind of Jew, and apparently my ex had made them. She had decided that she was the one kind and I was the other, lighter, more disposable kind. Long story short: she flew off to Lod. In retrospect, it was inevitable for her to so, as it was inevitable for me to drag my diaspora ass to New York.

II. Map of the World

In New York I cocooned myself in a tiny one-room apartment on 110th Street, with spiders in every corner and granite gargoyles lined up outside the window, and taught myself to write by the usual methods: trial, error, loneliness, humiliation. It took a long time but I had plenty of time, too much of it. I may have lacked everything else, but of time there was no shortage.

With a certain monklike devotion I burrowed in, davening over the altar of my desk, beseeching whatever invisible forces powered my hulking Selectric for knowledge I didn't have, guidance I was not yet ready to hear. That I had nothing to write *about* seemed a discouraging impediment, but I sensed opportunities lurking out of view, unassigned territories waiting to be claimed. Anyway I was used to that. Used to living in the future imperfect, readying for some Large Formless Challenge That Can't Be Named. That was the story of my life. The trick was to convert it from an affliction to a solution. To make my lack of coherence *a form* of coherence.

To take Kafka's mordant, witty lament—"What have I in common with the Jews? I have nothing in common even with myself"—and fashion from it my own little anti-national anthem.

The question was where to turn for help. Like a lot of Jewish-American writers of my generation, I tried to look past the usual suspects (Bellow, Roth, Malamud, Paley, Ozick, Singer, et al.) to other, more far-flung voices to which we were not as claustrophobically related. Borges, Marquez, Calvino, Yourcenar, Tanizaki, Duras, Boll, Naipaul . . . all appeared to offer an escape from those clingy, judgmental patriarchs and matriarchs of ours, in whose shadows we trembled. They loomed over us, ubiquitous and inescapable, as the shadow of Kafka's father loomed over him: *"At times I imagine the map of the world laid out, and you stretched across it. And all that is left for my life are the areas you don't cover or can't reach."*

Of course the Roths and Bellows and Malamuds, it should be noted, had their own Oedipal angels to wrestle with. *They* hadn't grown up reading Roth and Bellow and Malamud. They read Joyce, Flaubert, Dostoevsky, James, Tolstoy, Lawrence. Nor did they hang out in shul, murmuring liturgies and pieties with the faithful. That wasn't their scene. The actual *Jewishness* of the great Jewish-American laureates was, let's face it, more than a little notional to begin with. So where did that put us? Notions of notions. Vestiges of vestiges. The whole Jewish-American writer industry, by the time I came along, seemed to be running on fumes. That all-too-familiar hyphen had outlived its usefulness. (*"Foo to all these categories!"* says Moses Herzog.) How long did we have to keep looking over our shoulders anyway? The sea had been crossed long ago. We were free.

"The reason one becomes a poet," wrote Mandelstam's own ex-girlfriend, Marina Tsvetaeva, *"is to avoid being French, Russian, etc., in order to be everything."*

The only problem with freedom is you never get the right amount of it. Freedom to be anything began to bear a suspicious resemblance to freedom to be nothing. Neither felt too free at all.

What I am trying to say is that no matter how determined I was, in art and in life, to transcend my own origins, they kept tugging at me from behind, like the hands of an annoying sibling. At some point, I gave up even pretending to ignore them and took up what seemed like a transparently foolish project: a "Jewish-American novel" of my own. Whether this represented a victory over my ambivalences or a surrender to them was no longer possible, or even interesting, to sort out. By then it was impossible to write or even *think* the words "Jewish-American novel" without resorting to air quotes, maintaining some ironic separation from my own subject. And yet there I was, doing it anyway. Who knows why? There are ironies so commonplace they're hardy worth lingering over. In any case the question of motive had to be tabled—or if not tabled then absorbed like a blood stain into the fabric of the project—if I was ever to move forward with my story, the inspirations of which I hardly remember, about a feckless half-Jew who gets tangled up, more or less against his will, with a Hasidic couple from Crown Heights.

The composition process surprised me, as despite my internal resistance—or maybe because of it—the prose came very quickly. This seemed counterintuitive, as the book did not adhere to any of the novel-writing patterns I knew. It certainly was not a case of writing what you know. It was more like writing what you *don't* know, what you aren't sure you even *want* to know, about something you already on some level sort of do know, or half-know, but can't conceptualize, or express, or for that matter rouse yourself to give two shits about really. Talk about fun! Whether this maddening, Beckett-like uncertainty informs the writing of all novels, along with the drug and alcohol intake of all writers, I can't say. But it certainly informed mine.

Meanwhile there were other, extra-literary factors in the mix. By then I'd long since gone off and done it—fallen in love with a shiksa, exactly as my rabbi had feared. I'd wandered off the reservation, strayed over to the other side of the hyphen, the dark side. Another shallow-rooted diaspora Jew washed away in the flood. Go ahead and say it, Rebbe: I'd plunged that dagger right up my people's *kishkas*, into their bleeding heart.

Then too my wife was something of a poster child herself: blonde, blue-eyed, midwestern—the whole *shmeer*. A single mother, a child from a previous marriage, a gentile marriage no less. Now pregnant with our own son. Which meant, just in case I'd been in any doubt on the subject, I was now a walking, all but certifiable stereotype of assimilation.

The realization fell like a blow. *This* was what it meant to be Chosen: to have no choice. To say yes to one thing, I'd said no to another, and the binaries were closing in around me on all sides. There was no escape. Somehow, for all my attempts to wriggle free of that damned hypen, I'd wound up impaled on it instead.

Still, who could say? Everything was still in process. Maybe this half-Jewish kid of mine, like this half-Jewish novel I had only half-written, would be nurtured by these inner conflicts and dualities and somehow transform them, become the very vehicle of their transcendence. Wasn't that what kids and books were for? *"There are questions we would never get over were we not delivered from them by the operations of nature."* This wistful little aphorism of Kafka's we put on the birth announcement. Arguably there were less annoying, less pretentious ways to introduce one's son to the world. But the words appeared to be calling to us, choosing us, as we chose them.

III. The Damage

The thing about questions is there's never any end to them. And they're invariably rhetorical anyway.

Take that great late story by Donald Barthelme, "Chablis." It's five a.m., the narrator sits at his desk, smoking, worrying, sipping wine, looking out at the joggers "running towards rude red health" on the pre-dawn streets, and wonders, *"What's the matter with me? Why can't I be a more natural person?"* By "natural" he means someone more like the joggers and less like himself. Someone who doesn't sit around in the early morning, drinking and brooding and interrogating himself; someone whose nature and temperament is, in short, nothing like the narrator's at all. And yet it *seems* more natural, even to him, to be the person running out in the street, rather than the one watching from inside. (*"I stand between two worlds,"* says Mann's Tonio Kroger, nose pressed against the window, staring at the ruddy blonde folk dancing inside; *"I am at home in neither, and I suffer in consequence."*). The "natural" thing, we sense in our animal bones, is to transcend our contemplative inertia, and actually lace up our sneakers and go *do* something. *Commit* to something. But what?

This is the narrator's problem. It was more or less my problem too. How to establish a context in a culture of no context? How to plow your own ground in a zero-gravity field? At some point you start to run out of patience, just standing there that way, bumping your nose against the glass; it becomes an urgent necessity to smash your way through. Never mind the mess. Never mind the damage. The damage you're willing to pay for. In fact more than willing. The truth is, you *want* to pay.

By you, of course, I mean me, and by the damage, I mean that accursed Jewish-American novel of mine. Only when the book was in galleys did I chance to read Chaim Grade's story "My Quarrel With Hersh Rasseyner," and thereby discover that none of what I'd written was in any way new. It had all been done, with much greater acuity and concision, long before. But that too is an old story about stories. They've *always* been done before. Even the voice of the book, which I took to be so quirky and individual, seems to me now suspiciously crowd-sourced and familiar, a synthesis of all those noisy, Yiddish-inflected tonalities of my childhood, which I'd once found so vulgar, so suffocating, so antithetical to a life in art.

(Tsvetaeva again: "*Yet every language has something that belongs to it alone, that is it.*")

You say *Chosen*, I say *No Choice* . . . in the end, who knows, maybe it all comes to the same thing. We never escape our autobiographies. We never quite know what we're writing, but we never stop writing what we know. It so happens I *did*, once upon a time, find myself sitting next to a young Hasidic couple on a plane, very much like the protagonist of my novel, though unlike the novel nothing ever came of that conversation but an invitation to dinner I was never even tempted to take seriously at the time. Or it may not have been dinner. It may have been coffee. Who remembers? Maybe there was no invitation. Maybe there wasn't even a *plane*. All I know is I was in flight to somewhere, with an in no way metaphorical, half-Jewish creature kicking around in my wife's belly, asserting a few rights and claims of his own, so I started to play around a little, as writers do, with the what-ifs. I thought for some reason it would be a fun book to write. Or if not fun, then at least instructive. Or if not that either, at least a benign way of advancing the ball down the field, in that tediously protracted game of Ambivalence About Jewishness I'd been playing my whole life.

As it happened, it wasn't fun to write. It took me four years and eight or nine drafts, and no matter how much I worked, no matter how many fictionally interesting questions I spun around in my mind, no matter who I interviewed or how much Rashi and Buber and Scholem I read, that internal gate—behind which my soul lay sleeping—never quite sprang open. I never did resolve my Jewish problem. What happened instead was something more prosaic. I wrote a novel. Like most novels it was terribly flawed, and a good deal more persuasive in its questions than its answers. More an illustration of mixed feelings than a transformation of them. On the other hand mixed feelings, I've come to believe, are better than no feelings at all. I believe this the same way I believe everything else: partially, skeptically. Half yes and half no.

IV. Coda

The week that book came out I got a call from from the *Jewish Press*, asking for my thoughts on "the contemporary Jewish-American novel." I told the reporter I had both way too many thoughts on the subject and way too few, which was why I'd taken the trouble of writing my own novel in the first place. Nor was I comfortable, I said, labeling it a contemporary Jewish-American novel, even if it *was* contemporary, even if it *was* Jewish-American. I explained to the reporter, with a certain fastidious vehemence, how all such labels are dumb and reductive, and that, in my experience, any adjective you chose to append to a writer's name other than *brilliant* or *sexy* (ultimately of course one settles for *living*) feels like a crushing insult, and so on. This went on for a while. At last the reporter broke in to inform me, gently, that she really had to wind things up, because she had another piece to write too, a little sidebar that would run along with my interview, listing the ten most important Jewish-American writers of our time.

Wait, I said. *You mean there's a list of Jewish-American writers, and I'm not on it?*

But she had long since hung up.

A Maker of Mirrors

I am gazing, as I write, at a black and white photograph of Richard Fariña with his wife Mimi (née Baez) Fariña, taken backstage at the Newport Folk Festival nine months before his death—fifty years ago this week—at the age of twenty-nine. To call the photo romantic would be a ludicrous understatement. It's more like *ecstatic*. Mimi, her face upturned, a dark flower proffered to an invisible sun, appears to be literally bursting out of her flip-flops as she executes, with no apparent difficulty, some twirling, theatrical, Isadora Duncan-y ballet step. Beside her stands Richard, swarthy and black-haired, eyes fondly delta'd (even the Ray-Bans in his hand are useless in the face of this brightness), as if he can't quite believe his luck. This graceful, exuberant sprite, this radiant princess from folk's royal family, has joined her fortunes to his, or maybe vice versa. Anyway it's a nice day, and it's only the beginning: there are a lot more nice days to come.

Truth is, he's having a pretty good run of it for a guy who plays the dulcimer. And technically he doesn't even play it all that well. Still, something about the *way* he plays—his headlong, propulsive, feverishly percussive style, full of modal tones, Latin and Irish cadences—appears to endear him to the Newport people as original and fresh, as if the instrument is simply a natural extension of his own extravagant lyricism, prodigious charm, and sheer buoyancy of spirit. ("That was Fariña, man," one friend attested later, "you thought he was full of shit, then he delivered the goods and knocked everybody out.") He may not be a professional musician, but he must be an artist of *some* sort. Perhaps even, as David Hajdu suggests in *Positively 4th Street*, his group portrait of the early-sixties Village folk scene, an important one.

But *what* sort was he? Novelist? Poet? Songwriter? Bullshitter? None of this has made itself clear yet, that summer afternoon in Newport. And it's getting to be time. By now he's been performing, in one venue or another, for years—telling tales, fabulating adventures, improvising personae from the smoke and mirrors of his own mock-heroic (or maybe not so mock) bravado, and honing, it must be said, a gift for brazen opportunism along the way. Maybe that *is* his real talent. Not so much his impressive facility and work ethic, but something else too, some keen intuitive

Mimi and Richard Fariña at Newport. Copyright: 1965 David Gahr (Getty Images)

feel for the electric currents of his time, the roaring relays of its political and cultural energies, the flickering voltages of its tastes and styles.

It's one thing to be cool; it's another to be somehow *necessary*. A catalytic spark. A super-connector. A not-so-invisible bridge between the fifties and sixties. And in retrospect that's what Fariña was: a charismatic presence who for a brief, all too transient interval half a century ago, seemed to draw everything in his ambit into convergence. How fitting that someone so taken with comic book superheroes ("He walked and talked as if he had been born wearing a cape," a college friend tells Hajdu), would appear in retrospect a kind of superhero himself. A vaulter of skyscrapers, a spinner of webs, a lover of stars, and a colorful, boisterous influence on his many, many friends—including Bob Dylan and Thomas Pynchon, arguably the two foremost American artists of their generation.

Neither of whom are in Fariña's league, by the way, when it comes to sexual charisma. Or improvisory self-invention. Or a hunger for attention. Not least among his ambitions is Literary Fame. For years, he's been sort of dabbling and posing, hanging out at the White Horse with the other Dylan Thomas wannabes, but now he's working seriously and hard, trying to make good on the IOU of his promise. He's already sent off chapters of his novel-

in-progress to his Cornell pal Pynchon. He's published a few whimsical little poems and romantic, rain-soaked stories in literary magazines. Why
shouldn't he be a famous writer? He certainly *looks* the part, with his black
Byronic curls, his smoldering, half-Irish, half-Cuban intensity. Anyway
writing a novel isn't that hard: you just bluff your way in and make some
scenes. And Fariña's good at that. He's been making scenes everywhere he
goes, organizing protests at Cornell, busking his way through Europe, insin-
uating himself into the Village folk world, and now here he is, ascending
that triumphant summit, the stage at Newport. You can see the light bounc-
ing off the PERFORMER badge on his belt like a superhero's insignia.
What with his youth, his energy, his wit, his beauty (even the cleft that dim-
ples his chin winks like a grace note in the spotlight, the ornamental touch
of God's own finger) there's nothing to hold him back.

No one's surprised in the least when, a few months later, that first
novel of Fariña's gets published by Random House. Or that every copy he
signs, at his first and only book party in Carmel, is inscribed with the same
one word, written over the fly-leaf in an audacious, irresistible hand:
Zoom.

That six hours later Fariña will be dead in a motorcycle crash on Highway
1—killed in full *zoom*, as it were—is of course inconceivably tragic, and
might have affected me powerfully at the time had I any idea who he was.
But I was eight years old when he died, and it would be another six or
seven years before I happened to stumble upon a paperback of *Been Down
So Long It Looks Like Up to Me*, and a lifelong obsession kicked into gear.

I'd stumbled upon the book in the same way I stumbled on everything else that interested me in those days: by browsing my elder brother's
bookshelves for pornographic materials. Happily, the good people at Dell
had emblazoned the jacket with the outline of a rather fetching and apparently quite naked woman whose waterfalling hair and pale, sinuous geometries spoke of unspeakable enticements below the covers. *That* got my
attention. Then too the title, with its casually on-running lower-case font,
sounded like a line from a blues song I sort of thought I might have heard
once, though was not yet cool enough to identify. Possibly someday, with
the novel's instruction, I would become so. There was also a dumb but
jazzy tag-line in the description about how the novel would reveal the
concerns of "today's turned on, hung-up youth" (an odd claim for a book
that was actually set in the fifties, but never mind) along with a brief but
vivid author bio on the back—obviously written by the author himself—
which it would be criminal to paraphrase, so here it is in its entirety:

Richard Fariña was born of a Cuban father and Irish mother, both of whom came to this country during the thirties. He spent time with them in Brooklyn, Cuba, and Northern Ireland. At eighteen, he worked with members of the Irish Republican Army but eventually had to leave the country. Much the same for Cuba, which he visited often when Castro was still in the mountains, and again during the heavy fighting in Santa Clara and while the revolutionary army was entering Havana. After he left Cornell in '59 until late '63, he lived in London and Paris. The author writes that he made his living from "music, street singing, script-writing, acting, a little smuggling, anything to hang on. Lost thirty pounds."

It makes me laugh now, but Reader, listen: I believed every word. I *needed* to believe it. I was a fourteen-year-old kid in the suburbs: a failed athlete, an indifferent musician, an uninspired student, and a hopelessly impressionable romantic. I was desperate for a little audacity in my life. A little *life* in my life. I itched to smuggle and fight, to overthrow governments, to run out and roar with the big, cool cats. So far things did not look too promising in that department. There was very little running and roaring going on. All I had in my favor were the usual inflated dreams and sensitivities; an addiction to books, pot, and masturbation (in no particular order); and a modest reputation among my friends for gloomy wit, radical posturing, and formidable hair. Oh, and I sort of wanted to be a writer someday too.

I was still a little hazy on the details of what that last ambition entailed. At the time, I conceived of the writing life as a very serious but not entirely bookish vocation, with a lot of global travel and late night TV appearances and the occasional magazine cover, too. Which is to say, I conceived of it the way people do who never write a word.

But let's be clear: I didn't want to be just any writer, not even a writer like Richard Fariña. I wanted to *be* Richard Fariña. To *become* Richard Fariña. Because by then I'd read that first and only book of his six or seven times, to the exclusion of practically everything else I should have been reading; by then it had so thoroughly laid siege to my head, planted so many colored flags in my grey matter, that it was impossible to say where his sensibility left off and my own began. I was conversant with every move, every reference, every flourish. That's not to say I understood the book, in fact I probably didn't. But I absorbed it entirely.

And I didn't stop there, either. I wore out the grooves of the two gorgeous folk albums he'd made with Mimi. I snagged a copy of his not-entirely-publication-worthy posthumous prose, *Long Time Coming and A Long Time Gone*, and committed its whimsical little poems and transparently effortful pastiches of Dylan Thomas to memory. Basically I'd ceded over my imaginative life to Fariña, and felt in no particular hurry to get it back. (Not uncoincidentally, my own novice fiction, a few years later, would feature a number of brooding, Fariña-esque young men trying to charm a number of radiant, Mimi-ish waitresses in a number of dismal but atmospherically rain-battered Irish pubs). So why not surrender completely? I might as well go all-in, I thought: just go ahead and write Fariña's book, play Fariña's music, marry Fariña's wife, live Fariña's life, perhaps even die Fariña's death. But mostly, write Fariña's book. Which I hope I've made clear by now that I loved and admired, and took far too personally for my mental health.

That being said, the last thing I've wanted to do is re-read it as an adult, lest I discover that it was not in fact very good.

Now, with the book's 50th anniversary upon me, I *have* re-read it, and I'm relieved to report that it is in fact very good. Or pretty good. Or at least screwy and funny, and musically written, and often a little exasperating, and in the end, surprisingly dark, mordant, and acerb. At once a campus novel, a comic picaresque in the vein—the whole arm, really—of J. P. Donleavy's *Ginger Man*, and a *roman à clef* of Fariña's cohort at a barely-fictionalized Cornell, the book, like its hipster protagonist, Gnossos Pappadopoulis, postures and prances all over the place, tossing a lot of spaghetti against the wall, not all of which sticks. Still, it's a great deal of fun. The prose spritzes like a fountain, dispensing merry little streams of sex (polymorphous), drugs (hallucinogenic), cocktails (potent), jazzy hat-tips (Miles, Mose Allison), pop-cult invocations (Captain Midnight, The Shadow), revolutionary politics (Cuba), cartoony Pynchon-esque names (Louie Motherball, G. Alonso Oeuf, Oswald Mojo), and a vocabulary ("phthisic" anyone?) that seems determined to bring new meaning to the word "showy." And yet below that fizzy surface runs a deep current of dark energy, a paranoiac shadow, a barely-suspended malignancy of controlled chaos, and a sense of inevitable defeat, to which no one in the novel seems to be paying enough attention. (That the fifties were a boom time for American science fiction is no coincidence.) But it's thrumming along anyway, just out of view.

Gnossos is preternaturally attuned to these dark frequencies. Though he enters the novel in light, mock-heroic mode, a Odysseus returning from exotic adventures, "mind awash in schemes," his return to the campus proves no safe haven. Forces of evil, vaguely imperialist in nature, are massing like storm clouds just outside the gates. Everywhere he goes he finds traces of occult shadow, toxic emanation. In a contemporaneous song, "Children of Darkness," Fariña captures this transitional mood, this dawning awareness of insidious menace:

> It's once I was free to go roaming in
> The wind of the springtime mind
> And once the clouds I sailed upon
> Were sweet as lilac wine
> Then why have the breezes of summer, dear
> Enlaced with a grim design?

Onto this Manichean battlefield ambles Gnossos, our scruffy romantic superhero, in his usual armor of cool indifference, Teflon exemption ("I am not ionized," he boasts, "and I possess not valence") and impish contempt for authority. None of which prove adequate to protect him from what's going down. All the youthful bravado and careless ecstasies turn rancid. A friend is killed in Cuba; a letter from the draft board arrives; and ionized or not, Gnossos and his hip pals prove no more exempt from or immune to the corruptions of American life than the squares in the dorms. The book, which I remembered as a giddy, hypnagogic flight into sixties culture, ends surprisingly bitterly, on a resounding down note of defeat.

Possibly this was Fariña's intention all along: to sneak up on us, charm us with a bit of wine, whimsy and song, and then shoot us in the head. Or possibly his mood, in the six years it took to write, wandered and evolved, took a sharp turn for the bleak. Fifty years down the road, whose hasn't? Whatever the case, for all its antic high spirits and paregoric pleasures, the novel turns out to be kind of a bummer.

Also, just for the record: blatantly derivative (Donleavy's not the only one who could have filed charges); racially appalling (think Mickey Rooney in *Breakfast at Tiffany's*); way too full of glib, sonorous but dubious insights ("life is a celluloid passion"); and just generally riddled with what one character calls "a whole lot of doodley-shit." But so what? Like most good first novels, its flaws and excesses are inseparable from its appeal. It's a ride. A sonic adventure. And if like all functions of youth it's a bit too smugly pleased with its own intensity, and has yet to find or even look for, let alone concede, the outer limits of what it knows, and takes more pride than it should in its uncompromising perceptions and showy, sound-cloud atmospherics, we don't succumb to it in spite of these things, but because of them. "You want it all without the discipline," an older mentor figure tells Gnossos. Maybe the author was talking to, or about, himself a little too.

Anyway fair enough: the guy was only what, twenty-nine? Leave him alone. He was still finding his chops, forging his style; he had, there was every reason to think, plenty of time ahead to refine it.

"You know what I want to be when I grow up?" Gnossos asks at one point. "A maker of mirrors, that's what."

It's possible, had Fariña lived to write a sequel, that Gnossos would have gone on to serve in Vietnam. Or more likely fled to a commune in Western Canada where, blissed out like Doonesbury's Zonker (to whom he bears no little resemblance) he'd pass his days nibbling feta and sipping retsina, tending his own lush, fragrant garden. But more likely his creator would have ditched him. And not just him. Indeed, Fariña seems a writer capable of ditching the novel game altogether. I could imagine him doing a lot of other things: acting in movies, taking up yoga, teaching himself the oboe, or maybe wandering a few miles over from Carmel to the flatlands of Cupertino, where he'd develop some weird new computer code, one that braided all previous computer codes together in some intriguingly imaginative, highly lucrative way. Any future for a guy of his talents, had he lived, seems equally plausible, with the possible exception of the most realistic one: the eighty year old man he'd be now, with thinning hair, aching joints, and a trainload of memories and regrets.

But of course Fariña didn't live. He died in his twenties. Which means he'll forever remain as he was, haloed in promise, suspended in youth's amber, forever exempt—Gnossos' favorite word—from the prosaic mediocrity and disappointments of a long, pretty good life. If that offers any compensation, it's not for Fariña to enjoy. It's for the rest of us.

For me, back in 1972, that early death seemed all too ominous. It was a very paranoid time. Some vast subterranean conspiracy appeared to be at work, some evil *counter*-counter-culture of Nixonian technocrats pulling levers behind dark curtains, stomping down protests and idiosyncrasies, snuffing out hard, gemlike flames, and because I fancied at the time that I might be nurturing one of those flames myself, way down deep, I took Fariña's fate weirdly personally. I took his death personally. I took his life personally. I took his work and music personally. I took the intense, personal feelings these things evoked in me personally. The intersecting parabolas of all that youthful feeling, his and mine, against a background of what seemed its own forever war, the apprehension of an early death that seemed poised out there somewhere beyond the insulations of the suburbs, waiting to spring . . . all this converged in me, forming a blurry malignant shape that looked, to me anyway, like the tragic and impersonal geometry of the adult world. A net with more holes than string.

Still, those strings do surprise you. Their strength and buoyancy, their stubborn resilience. Even half a century later you can look down and there they are, still holding you up.

C. and Sardinia

"*I don't care for islands,*" D. H. Lawrence once wrote, an attitude I happen to share by the way, though my wife doesn't, which long story short is how we wound up spending six months in Sardinia.

Whether Lawrence himself shared it, given his habit of asserting cranky and intemperate opinions he only fleetingly believed, isn't clear. At that time in his short, peripatetic life—winter, 1921—it was pretty much islands all the way down. He was living on one island (Sicily), in exile from another (England), and about to embark upon an impromptu whirlwind trip to a third (Sardinia). Trips of this kind were a Lawrentian specialty, despite the fact, or because of it, that he did not much care for travel either. But he needed to go *some*where. He had a restless nature, a discomfort in his own skin, and a seemingly perpetual need for release from—and/or a productive channel for—that febrile, prodigious whirlwind he carried around in his head. So why *not* Sardinia?

In any case his stay there, however brief and unsatisfying, would go on to yield one of his most original and peculiar books. If *Sea and Sardinia* is, on some level, a pretty ragged and minor work, it may be the kind of ragged, minor work only a major novelist can produce. It occupies a rather unique place in the modern library. As does the man who wrote it, of course. You can hear him muttering in there even now, at once resigned to being ignored and compulsively complaining about it, refusing to sit quietly or leave.

It all begins with that jittery, bewitching opening line: "*Comes over one an absolute necessity to move.*" For Lawrence, life's too short and art too long to fuss over syntax; he's too impatient to get going to waste time on the niceties, too enthralled by the prospect of movement to wonder where it's taking him, toward or from. There's only one thing that aggravates him more than travel ("*traveling is usually a misery*"), and that's staying put. Staying home. *What* home? Lawrence *has* no home. He *wants* no home. The indoor life, the settled life, the reflective life, the analytical life . . . aren't these the very qualities of sickly, pallid, cosmopolitan Europe, and of himself too, he's most desperate to escape?

"*Life itself would be in the flight*," he thinks, boarding the ferry in Palermo. "*The tremble of space.*"

Of course wherever he goes he expects, as most of us do, way too much. Consequently he's always disappointed. But also enlivened. Because the toxic cloud of that disappointment—the acid rain of insults, sudden rages, and random kvetches and complaints—as it splatters percussively across the page, keeps soaking into the imagery, heightening and distorting the impressions, making everything vivid, undeniable, and intense. Disappointment tends to bring out the best of Lawrence. Also the worst of Lawrence. Admittedly, these two categories are often indistinguishable. Lawrence in a bad mood, and he's never far from one, can sound tiresome and silly and shrill; though it's also true that bad moods elevate his game, as steroids do for athletes: the swing is the same but the ball travels farther, with greater velocity and spin.

The trajectory of the resulting prose can sink you to your knees. Take this typically glancing but stunning description: "*In the bar the wretched candle was weeping light.*" Note how the wretchedness of the candle and the gorgeousness of that "weeping light" emanate from the same source, which has little to do with the setting per se and everything to do with the man who observes it. Whatever his vague intentions in coming to Sardinia, this is arguably the real goal: this generating of heightened perception, heightened attunement, heightened prose. And if the portrait of Sardinia that results bears less resemblance to the actual place than to that other supremely prickly and forbidding body, Lawrence himself? So be it. Lawrence doesn't care. Anyway the novelist, in his view, "is usually a dribbling liar." God knows he's no stranger to the many impurities and betrayals that result from an attempt to translate reality into art:

> When van Gogh paints sunflowers, he reveals, or achieves, the vivid relation between himself, as man, and the sunflower, as sunflower, at that quick moment of time. His painting does not represent the sunflower itself. We shall never know what the sunflower itself is . . . the vision on the canvas is for ever incommensurable with the canvas, or the paint, or van Gogh as a human organism . . . it is neither man-in-the-mirror nor flower-in-the-mirror . . . it is in between everything, in the fourth dimension.

So too with Lawrence's travel writings. Place is more the vehicle for the portrait than the destination. After all, as he reminds us, he's "not Baedeker." He's not even all that *interested* in Sardinia, I don't think. He's just a freelance wordsmith with too much time on his hands, and no children at home—no *home* at home—to occupy it.

In short, something of a dilettante. After all he spends only nine days on the island total. He takes no notes; he manages to neglect or avoid most of the (admittedly few) historical sites; he's a fidgety, inattentive tourist, an ungracious guest, a slapdash journalist who shamelessly repeats himself, contradicts himself, and essentializes people about whom he knows nothing (he likes to refer to the black-haired, black-eyed natives as "Eskimos"). Every sketch he draws is a little wild, a little monstrous. He tends to color not just outside the lines but off the paper and over the walls. He's one of those guys who can't bear to wait in line. He's always *lurching ahead, pushing past,* trying to see better, to *seize hold* of some stony, inhospitable truth around the corner—the kind of truth one either grasps very quickly or not at all. That the majority of these truths turn out to be more projected than discovered does nothing to diminish the force with which they're expressed. *"The judgment may be all wrong,"* he concedes at one point. *"But this was the impression I got."*

Fortunately Sardinia is accustomed to putting up with, and shrugging off, the transient fervor of other people's impressions. The Greeks called the place *Ichnusa,* meaning "footprint." Having finished creating the earth (goes the origin story), God gathered up the leftover pieces of rock, tossed them into the sea, and stomped down with his heel. *Et voilà*: Sardinia. This appears to have set a certain precedent, as haughty and ill-mannered intruders have been hoofing it over the island ever since. The Phoenicians, the Carthaginians, the Athenians, the Romans, the Vandals, the Pisans, the Catalans; billionaire yachtsmen, media moguls, Eurotrash, crabby and indolent novelists, it never ends. When you're smack in the middle of the Mediterranean, blessed with fertile slopes, gorgeous views, flawless beaches, and easy Ryanair connections, you get no shortage of visitors.

And yet the island, like most islands, retains its own rarefied air of apartness. Topographically, politically, linguistically, maybe even characterologically. There's a palpable intransigence, a sense of stubborn detachment Lawrence seemed to recognize and be drawn to, as one is drawn to a mirror. *"Lost between Europe and Africa and belonging to nowhere."* He might as well be talking about himself.

What is the man after, on these Italian journeys? What does he expect to find? To what does he hope to lay claim? *"An unknown, unworked land where the salt has not lost its savor"* is the closest he can come to naming it. He's arrived there, like an investigator at an arson site, to sift through the

ashes, hunting for some smoldering, half-buried clue, some as yet unextin-
guished ember—pre-modern, pre-Christian, maybe even pre-*human*—
something to reveal the full scope of the crime, and indict his arch enemy,
so-called "civilization," for good. But the answer eludes him.

"*There is an uncaptured Sardinia still,*" he encourages himself. "*It lies
within the net of this European civilization, but it isn't landed yet.*"

Which he desires more—to land the place in the net of his prose, or
be reassured that he can't—it's hard to say. Like any serious artist, he's torn
between the desire to impose his will on reality and the equal-and-
opposite desire for a reality that refuses to yield. Think of Cézanne out
there sketching Mount St. Victoire day after day, irresistibly drawn to its
stubborn and impersonal defiance, its refusal to sit still for its own portrait. And yet he goes on sketching it anyway, unable or unwilling to stop.

We're unable to stop either, my wife and I. We have, during our extended
residence on the island, launched our own semi-obsessive quest through
Sardinia, following Lawrence and Frieda's footprints—that blotchy, ser-
pentine ink-trail—wherever they lead. Like all literary pilgrimages it
seems, once begun, a little random and pointless even to us. Nonetheless
I've committed to doing an article on the subject, and so am now, for
better or worse, contractually obligated to go ahead.

Already on day one there are problems. My license having expired
while we're abroad, my wife is forced to take over the driving, which
immediately puts us both outside our comfort zones. Little snorts of tension and suppressed resentment leak from the driver's seat as she shifts
into gear, navigating perilous mountain switchbacks. Meanwhile over in
the passenger's seat it's all I can do to jot down a few rudimentary notes
without throwing up. Clearly this project of tracking Lawrence in motion
is destined to be a demanding, wearying affair. And we haven't even gone
anywhere yet.

On the other hand, tracking Lawrence *on* motion is no picnic either.
He's as hasty and erratic on the page as he is in life. In both venues there's
a surfeit of volatile, manic-depressive mood swings. He's always zigzagging between extremes, oscillating between moments of sudden exal-
tation (the movement of a ship, the wildness of a landscape, the generosity
of a peasant) and sputtering exasperation (almost everything else). If not
for Frieda's calming influence, who knows how he would have managed.
But thankfully she was, as always, along for the ride. Indeed were it not for
her teasing, almost loftily stabilizing presence (Lawrence refers to her in
the book as "Q-B," for Queen Bee) and her warm, infectious enthusiasm

for the island and its people, we'd be tempted to ditch Lawrence *and* his book by the side of the road. But the Q-B acts as a kind of designated driver, cheerfully ignoring the ruckus around her, adeptly maneuvering the vehicle of the journey forward.

My own companion (I have permission, for alliterative purposes only, to call her "C.") lines up firmly with Team Frieda by the way. Immediately upon landing in Cagliari she declares herself in love. And not with me. It's the gleaming porticos of the Via Roma, the palm-lined walkways, the stately Pisan towers hovering like sentinels over the rooftops, the shops filled with wild asparagus, long-stemmed artichokes, plump and shiny fennels and figs . . . all evoke in her an almost savage sensual delight. Lawrence for his part finds the town, as he finds most towns, wanting. "All bibs and bobs," he comments, "rather bare, rather stark." Most of his time there is spent complaining about the cold, ignoring the people, and just generally dodging slop-water on all sides.

But Frieda is very much in her element here ("Oh, if I don't live at Cagliari, and come and do my shopping here," she exclaims, "I shall die with one of my wishes unfulfilled") and so, a century later, are we. True, much of the architecture is undistinguished at best, the facades of the buildings saggy and wan, pockmarked with dark vacancies. But that's hardly Cagliari's fault—its downtown was leveled back in the war, in the course of one hot July night, by Allied bombs. Naturally the local government has no money and is, well, a local Italian government, so it's not exactly an immaculate, orderly city. The tourist trade is flagging, the cruise ships have all deserted to Barcelona, the historical sites, such as they are, look poorly maintained, the flights from Rome on Alitalia are nowhere near full. But Cagliari's hanging in there anyway. It's been here three thousand years. It has an unfussy, lived-in air all its own, an affect of weathered survival and convivial endurance. In the evenings people lounge on rooftops, sipping Day-Glo orange Aperol Spritzes from enormous bowl-shaped glasses. From the heights of the Bastione di San Remy the entire bay can be seen, laid out in the twilight: freighters idling in port, the distant salt flats, peppered with pink flamingos, the long flat city beach, the Poetto, unfurling like a moonscape beyond. Couples stroll the Via Manno, savoring their *passagiatas*, making out languidly under the waving palms. "They pour themselves one over the other," Lawrence sniffs, "like so much melted butter over parsnips." For an alleged sensualist he's really quite the prig. But that's one of the tragedies of exile: you're never as free as you think from the provincial bonds you have and have not left behind.

After a few days, there being "little to see" in Cagliari, the Lawrences move on to Mandas, some seventy kilometers north. Honestly, there's no particular reason for *anyone* to go to Mandas. But having missed the direct train to Oristano he and Frieda are forced to take the secondary railway, the *Trenino Verde*—a quaint, toylike little choo-choo, one that crawls along so slowly that the thirty-five-mile trip to Mandas takes them six and a half hours.

Fortunately we're spared this particular aggravation, because the Trenino Verde, it turns out, no longer operates in low season. Also we've rented a car. Renting a car has been a controversial decision, not just because of the expense, and my license issues, and C.'s hatred of driving, but because the luxury of a car represents a clear betrayal of Lawrentian values—namely hardship, hunger, bad light, and the sharing of cramped, claustrophobic spaces with unattractive people whose proximity annoys you.

On the other hand, it's an enormous convenience to have a car, especially going to Mandas. The drive takes less than an hour, and I feel smug and happy the whole way. There are luminous views out the window of the Trexenta foothills, a gentle, undramatic landscape of olive trees and flowering almonds and pale, droopy-barked stands of eucalyptus, and the sheep outnumber the people, and it's all very placid and serene, a promise of good things to come. Even the clouds seem content, drifting along benignly overhead, puffy and light.

When we get to Mandas however there's not much doing. It's a bare, stony little village with treeless streets and no sidewalks to speak of. When cars and scooters whoosh past we're forced to dive for dear life against the walls of the stone houses. That seems to be the principle activity here in Mandas, dodging scooters. To dislocate your shoulder is a form of local entertainment. The Lawrences, having arrived in Mandas, asked the natives what there was to see. "*Niente*," they were told. "At Mandas one does *nothing*. At Mandas one goes to bed when it's dark, like a chicken. At Mandas one walks down the road like a pig that is going nowhere. At Mandas a goat understands more than the inhabitants understand. At Mandas . . ." and so on.

This isn't quite fair of course. There are *some* things to do in Mandas, according to our host there, a lean, warmly congenial fellow named Agostino, who runs our *locanda*. The inn, a converted staging post, has been in his family since Lawrence's day. In fact the "quite pleasant woman with the tight brown velveteen bodice" who tended to Lawrence and Frieda's (apparently near-bottomless) needs was, he informs us proudly, his own grandmother, Dondina Lunetta, from whom the locanda took its name.

He shows us her picture: a handsome, rather beleaguered looking woman, worn out by the burdens of hospitality. We nod pleasantly, and ask where to eat. But Agostino isn't finished. Are we interested in D. H. Lawrence? Do we know about the Festival D. H. Lawrence, he wants to know, a landmark celebration which takes place every August, with guests from all over the world? Do we want some brochures to take back with us? Should he go ahead and reserve space for us here at the locanda, as the rooms for the event will surely book fast?

When we inform Agostino that we're leaving in June and hence unable to attend the Festival, he smiles pleasantly, as if we have said in fact said something entirely different, though a thin membrane of judgment flicks down over his gaze. Here he thought we were Lawrence people: serious, passionate, committed. But apparently we're just casual tourists who don't give a damn. All we care about is food? Fine, go have food. He waves his wrist in dismissal, and sends us off to try the *agriturismo* down the road, which he recommends to all his boarders. I can see he's sorry to have entrusted us with his goddamn brochures.

We head over to try our luck. That we're the only customers in the place on a Friday evening seems oddly fitting, as there *are* no other boarders at the locanda. Have there *ever* been? Maybe it's just the Lawrences and us, two couples a century apart. God knows it's begun to feel that way.

Though the Lawrences, in the impoverished Mandas of 1921, can score nothing to eat but cabbage soup and hard bread, I'm pleased to report C. and I feast like Vikings that evening. Enormous *antipastis* of olives, pickled vegetables, prosciuttos, salamis, and pecorinos; *primis* of *culurgiones* (potato-and-mint-filled pasta dumplings); suckling pig and savory mutton; and *seadas*—hubcap-sized raviolis stuffed with fresh ricotta, deep fried in olive oil, and drizzled copiously with dark, bitter local honey—for dessert. Then we stagger back to the locanda and collapse on the bed. We decide, as we stare stupefied at the ceiling, that we've collapsed on the very bed on which the Lawrences once collapsed, staring up at the very ceiling the Lawrences once collapsed under. The kind of dumb little flight of magical thinking of which literary pilgrimages are made.

The next morning however, in one of those irritating little setbacks of which literary pilgrimages are also made, Agostino confirms this isn't true. It can't be, he informs us coolly, as the locanda's original location was a few blocks away next to the train station. To earn back some respect in his eyes, we head off there after breakfast. It's as if certifying the real, authentic site is some essential and important task. Of course like most real, authentic sites it turns out to be not much to look at. Just a deserted stone building of no particular interest, locked up tight. There's a small plaque on the façade dedicated to *Largo David Herbert Lawrence*, so I dutifully take a photo of that. Then we walk over to the little train station, where we discover not one but two additional Lawrence plaques, so I dutifully take photos of those too.

"It seems an awful lot of plaques," C. observes. "I mean he only spent one night here, and he did nothing but complain the whole time." Clearly spending time in Lawrence's company is rubbing off on her; her own complaints are multiplying by the hour. "What's up with that?"

"They like to honor their writers here. Remember that Cervantes plaque in Cagliari, next to the historical museum? And all *he* did was sail by one day on his way to somewhere else."

"That's what I mean. It's a bit weird."

"Maybe. But a lot of countries just ignore writers completely. I prefer it this way."

C. frowns. I can see she's tempted to say what she's thinking: that some writers get ignored more than others. Or is that just what *I'm* thinking? Clearly no matter how much time I squander here in Mandas, trudging down the stark, treeless streets, no matter how many notes I scribble or photos I take, there won't be any plaques to *me*.

Heading north we stop off at Su Nuraxi, a sprawling Stone Age complex of massive, hive-shaped stone towers. Apparently tens of thousands of these structures (in Italian: *nuraghi*) lie buried around the island. Of these Su Nuraxi is the largest to be excavated. Whatever its original purpose may have been—fortress, trading spot, sacred burial ground—it appears to have evolved over the centuries into a cosmopolitan city, its vast network of residential dwellings, cisterns and wells, atriums, grain mills, and canals forming the hub of an intricate, endemic culture roughly contemporaneous with Stonehenge.

In short, it's exactly the sort of place Lawrence came to Sardinia to find. A pulsing, pagan heart laid bare beneath the calcified crust. A "real thing" that would *"go off with a pop . . . and smash our mechanical oneness into smithereens."*

Sadly he never found it. Su Nuraxi, as things turn out, was not yet excavated in 1921. What he found instead was very different. What he found instead was Sorgono.

"Blessed is he that expecteth nothing," Lawrence says of Sorgono, *"for he shall not be disappointed."*

It began, like most of his beginnings, with great promise. The road through the Gennargentu mountains—called the *Barbagia* by the Romans, in deference to its scrubby, invasion-unfriendly wildness—writhes through a landscape of chestnuts, dwarf oaks, and half-stripped cork trees ("like coffee-brown, naked aborigines"). Ancient-looking shepherds in wool caps and corduroy trousers stand planted along the slopes. The sullen gongs of sheep-bells echo down the ravines. Life as it was. Nothing appeals to Lawrence more than life as it was.

But then one arrives in Sorgono, and what does he find? No life at all. More *niente*. "A dreary hole! A cold, hopeless, lifeless, Saturday afternoon-weary village, rather sordid, with nothing to say for itself." The food is meager. The bedsheets are stained. The local sport seems to be cheerfully relieving yourself against the walls of the houses. In the bar, that wretched, miserable candle, weeping inadequate light. "Why are you so indignant?" the Q-B demands of him, a little indignant herself at this point. "It's all life."

But indignation is Lawrence's default mode, in the same way discomfort is his comfort zone, and he's not about to abandon either one of them here in Sorgono. Indeed, no less than fourteen pages of the Sardinia book are devoted to his brief stay in "this vile village," every one spittled with invective about the (generally rather petty) discomforts he's forced to endure there, and honestly if I had my way there would be fourteen more. *This* is the Lawrence I love most: the unloved, unlovable Lawrence. The knight suited up for battle, who tilts headlong at every windmill, declares war on every enemy, whether an enemy exists or not. And on himself too. Himself too. This mess of bipolar contradictions, this savage bohemian who wants to be comfortable and well-fed; this humorless prig who wanders the world decrying humorlessness and priggishness; this transcendental visionary forever accumulating earthly grievances; this brilliant perceiver whose twitchy, sensitive feelers for the vagaries of nature seem incapable of doing justice to his own . . . all these embattled Lawrences come to the fore here in Sorgono, and cram those fourteen pages with almost more intensity of feeling than fourteen pages can bear.

C. and I have issues of our own by the way, where Sorgono is concerned. We too, like the Lawrences, arrive half-starved on a Saturday afternoon to find absolutely *niente* in evidence. Dark clouds have lowered over the surrounding mountains like some judgment of heaven, obliterating the daylight. The only restaurant that looks in any way open is also, confusingly, half-closed. We hear the murmur of voices inside but no host or staff comes to greet us; they're all ensconced in some other room, preparing for some elaborate party to which we're not invited. We seat ourselves at a conspicuous table, and settle in to wait. When at last a waiter happens by, seemingly by accident, he pretends to listen for a while to the peremptory, barking sounds of my restaurant Italian, which only vaguely approximate the names of actual Sardinian foods. Then he disappears. When he returns some time later he's carrying two not very full plates of pasta, leftovers, apparently, from the staff lunch. "And everyone says it's impossible to get a bad meal in Italy," I say to C., signaling for the check, which comes to forty euros we don't have. I'm forced to go out stomping through the streets of Sorgono—make that *street* of Sorgono—looking for the town's lone ATM. Naturally it's begun to pour.

C., for her part, withdraws to a covered bench by the lifeless station, where she quietly weathers the storm as she awaits or maybe dreads my return. She's in no mood for negative energy, and I appear to have a great deal of it here in Sorgono. Have I caught some kind of noxious infection from Lawrence? The anxiety of influence has gotten way out of hand.

In any event there's nothing to do but wait it out, sit there in the rain, staring at the faded pink façade of the decaying old building across the street, as if willing it to metamorphize into something more interesting, more promising. The name over the door—*Hotel Risveglio*—seems to me significant. I faintly recognize it from somewhere, perhaps a dream, perhaps another, better life. But why? Idly I turn the now-dampened pages of the Lawrence book, skimming over the Sorgono chapter for the third time. And there it is: the same name, the same hotel, the same "great, pink-washed building facing the station lane" where he and Frieda passed the dreariest, most lamentable night of their entire Sardinian journey.

"What are the odds? The worst hotel in town, and a century later it's still going."

"Maybe it's not the worst," C. says. "Maybe it's the only."

"Good point. What tourist in their right mind would ever come to stay here?"

"*We* came to stay here," C. observes mildly.

Yet another good point. We sit there in silence for a while, listening to the rain until it stops.

"Well," I say, stretching, "there must be a plaque around here somewhere. Should we go take a look?"

We cross the street. A number of brawny young men loiter idly outside the hotel, smoking cigarettes and sipping long-necked bottles of Ichnusa, the local beer. All of them are wearing the same vaguely menacing expression, the same military faux-hawks and black nylon tracksuits. Possibly the gang they belong to requires them not just to smoke and drink and intimidate strangers together but to get their clothes and haircuts together too. "Maybe we should pass," I say. "I don't love the looks of these guys."

"Don't be silly," C. says. Having grown up in Texas and given birth to two boys, these guys don't intimidate her in the least. If anything, it's the other way around. They part like a sea at her approach, then file in behind her through the front door, lining up at the bar like extras in an old spaghetti western (many of which were filmed, we discovered, not far away). A pallid, unfriendly looking gent in his thirties stands behind the bar, polishing glasses with a filthy cloth. Like any good cowpoke I slap down a euro and request, in my grunting, atrocious Italian, a couple o' macchiatos for me and the lady. He gives a grudging nod. Then, over the pulverizing roar of the coffee grinder, I ask if this happens to be the same Hotel Risveglio the famous British author D. H. Lawrence once patronized back in 1921.

For a moment he just stares at me. Whether it's my accent, my syntax, or my vocabulary that offends him isn't clear. Or maybe it's Lawrence himself, who repeatedly slandered this guy's beloved hometown as *a dreary hole*. Possibly, unlike those wimps down in Mandas, the Sorgonoites (Sorgonians?) have a zero-tolerance, zero-commemorative-plaques policy for all things Lawrence. Anyway it's an awkward moment. I glance over my shoulder, eyeing the exit path to the door just in case.

At last C. steps forward and explains, in her own quite *good* Italian, what it was I was trying to say.

All at once, as if a switch has been thrown, everybody starts talking at once. D. H. *Lawrence? Of course* they know D. H. Lawrence! Who in Sardinia *doesn't* know the great D. H. Lawrence? Why, it was the grandmother of this very bartender who attended to the man's needs here at the Risveglio! Or was it his *great*-grandmother? Or wait, didn't the great-grandmother sell the place to someone *else* back in 1919? It's all very confusing, very subject to historical interpretation and revision, and everyone in the bar has their own comment or factoid or rumor to contribute, and though I personally understand almost none of it, the pleasure it gives them, batting around the question and drinking a shitload of beer on a rainy afternoon, is considerable.

Like all Italian-language conversations, it goes on for a long time. At last, hoping to resolve the matter for good, I pull out my copy of the Lawrence book and lay it down on the bar, like a straight at the end of a tense round of poker. The bartender frowns. His dark eyes narrow. Then *he* reaches below the bar, produces *his* copy of the Lawrence book (*Mare e Sardegna*), and lays it down over mine like a flush. Busted! Everyone laughs, at whom it isn't clear. What difference does it make? Another round of Ichnusas for our own little Festival D. H. Lawrence!

By the time we're done toasting to things—to the Lawrences, to each other, to ourselves, to Sorgono—and at last take our leave of the Risveglio (our repeated attempts to pay for the drinks are waved off), the sky has cleared, the sun bathes the wildflowers in golden light, and Sorgono itself seems the coziest, most charming Sardinian village imaginable. Not that we have any intention of staying the night.

Buoyed by Ichnusa, and our small, unexpected success on the Lawrence trail, we zip up and down the mountain passes, headed towards Nuoro. The landscape is a marvel. Here are the high "sun-sweetened" villages like Gavoi and Tonara (where the nougat is made) with their "bright, flashing air," which the Lawrences admired from their seats on the bus. Ancient cork trees line the road, ruddy and fierce. The air stings our faces, the light is slanting and strong, the shop-windows gleam with refracted light. We pass half a dozen knife stores along the way, the blades laid out like cutlery, polished to a shine.

"This used to be *banditi* country," I tell C.

"Oh?"

"Don't worry. That stuff's over. They're all long retired."

"Ah." She points at a passing road sign, pocked by gouges and graffiti and wait, are those *bullet holes*? "So nothing to worry about, then."

"Probably just bored kids having fun."

"I notice they only shot up the English and Italian words. They didn't touch the Sardo."

"That's a relief." I pause a moment. "How *is* your Sardo anyway?"

Her hands tighten on the wheel. I can see that the high spirits with which we departed Sorgono have now taken a hit.

The rest of the way to Nuoro C. broods in silence, glaring at the road, offering me and any passing banditi foolish enough to fuck with her a view of her handsome, resolute profile.

Nuoro when we arrive looks to be a typical medium-sized Sardinian town, which is to say there's little to interest a casual tourist. Fortunately, C. and I are not casual tourists. On the other hand we can't find much to interest us either, aside from a brief visit to the birthplace of Grazia Deledda, the first female Nobel Laureate in literature, whose work Lawrence greatly admired. To our shame, neither of us has read her, or even heard of her. Still, as Sardinia's lone bona fide homegrown literary celebrity, she doubtless merits a few plaques of her own. But when we arrive at the tiny, none-too-promising museum of her birthplace, it is, in keeping with the rest of our journey, totally closed.

Now what? We walk aimlessly around the village for an hour or two, trying to see the place through Lawrence's eyes. Though of course in Lawrence's eyes, as he never tires of reminding us, "There's nothing to see." No, Nuoro through Lawrence's eyes is just another grey, cheerless town with one lousy café, a piazza like "a formless gap," and no cheese in the restaurants. Whether or not this remains true—there *is* cheese in the restaurants, though none of them are open; there's also a modest museum of modern art, or maybe a modern museum of modest art; anyway, a place to see art, which isn't open either—isn't the point. Odds are it wasn't true in Lawrence's day. The point is he wasn't looking. Indeed, the phrase "Nothing to see" pops up so often in *Sea and Sardinia* it begins to sound like some dour, depressive mantra, an all-purpose caption for whatever picture Lawrence happens to be looking at, or more to the point not looking at. If you don't bother to look, you can't be disappointed by what you do or don't see. Or to put it another way, he hopes for so much meaning from a place that he can't possibly receive it. But that hope must be preserved, that romantic innocence defended at all costs.

"Sights are an irritating bore," he declares. "Life is life and things are things. Happy is the town that has nothing to show." A nice new slogan for the Nouro tourist board.

Having unburdened himself of this sour little aperçu, the rest of the trip proves, in that sense anyway, a happy one for Lawrence. Because there's not much to see in *any* of these towns. In "dilapidated, sun-smitten, godforsaken little" Orosei; in huddled, stony "I can't say much for Siniscola" Siniscola; and finally in Olbia itself (Terranova in the book), which a century ago was a humdrum, sparsely populated port "more like a settlement than a town," but has now morphed into a blandly prosperous, self-satisfied little city—the gateway to the glittering shores of the Costa Smeralda, where shirtless capitalists pad around on their yachts, clinking slender flutes of prosecco as the sun dotes benevolently upon their shoulders. Had such resorts existed in Lawrence's day, he would have loathed them ferociously. And he would have loathed Olbia too, for its unctuous surrender to commerce, its belching ferries and swank boutiques and overpriced hotels. No, towns like Olbia were definitely not Lawrence's thing.

What *was* the man's thing anyway? Where was he going? What did he want? The longer we follow him the less we understand his "savage pilgrimage" through Italy, Malta, and Provence; through Ceylon and Australia; Mexico and New Mexico (had there been a *New* New Mexico, no doubt he'd have gone there too). Philip Larkin, in his "Poetry of Departures," writes of a man who walks away from domestic life, "This audacious, purifying/Elemental move." Maybe that's what it comes down to. If there are two essential modes, the settled and the unsettled, and the former is more congenial to the patient and the prosaic, and the latter to the poetic, to quick, jittery impressions and sudden bursts of feeling, then it's clear which way Lawrence's temperament inclined him. The hard way. The restless way. The nervy, unappeasable way. And if his reward for that life was a shortened, cantankerous existence full of rogue antagonisms and a shelf full of messy, smoldering compositions that will be read and argued over, when they're not being glibly dismissed, a hundred years later, maybe that's a trade-off he was willing to make. Certainly he paid the price for it. While we, who paid nothing, get the goods.

And the goods are considerable. The goods are astonishing. There's more good in those goods, in my view, more radiant intensity and seething perception, more swarming animation, more feverish concentration, than most of us will ever know in our lifetimes, on the page or off.

On the other hand, it all gets a bit exhausting after a while, too.

The truth is after a week or so we've sort of had it, C. and I, with the whole Lawrence-of-Sardinia business. No longer, as we drive, do I keep the book open on my lap, hectoring C. with his pedantic observations. No longer does she pretend to listen. Silently we wind up and down the coastal roads, the dust rising in clouds behind us, feeling at once weary and depleted and more than a little relieved, like Zen archers who have laid down their arrows and turned away from the target, ready to go home.

Then I hear C. let out a gasp. "Pull over," she says.

"Why?"

"Look."

And suddenly there it is in front of us, looming through the mist like an apparition: Tavolara.

Ahead we saw the big lump of the island of Tavolara, a magnificent mass of rock which fascinated me by its splendid, weighty form. It looks like a headland, for it apparently touches the land. There it rests at the sea's edge, in this lost afternoon world. Strange how this coast-country does not belong to our present-day world.

Has *this* has been Lawrence's destination—and ours—all along? This massive lump of limestone stranded in the middle of the Gulf of Olbia like some decrepit, fallen moon? The cliffs look unscalable. The summit lies shrouded in a pale, sinuous wreath of clouds it wears like a crown. Nothing that is human can be seen on it: no roads, no bridges, no stores, no restaurants. Like Su Nuraxi, it might be the abandoned remnant of some ancient, less user-friendly world. We pull over and stare at it for a while, wordlessly. There's nothing to say. If awe is a temporary separation from time, a reminder of human transience in the face of an impersonal and preexistent reality, then that's what it feels like at that moment, gazing at Tavolara. As if the line between inquisitive subject and indifferent object has blurred to the vanishing point.

That's my description by the way, not Lawrence's, even if that line too has begun to blur. Well, so what? Nothing wrong with that. Doubtless he too brought along books by other people, Grazia Deledda for instance, which colored not just what but how he saw. That's how these pilgrimages go. The wider you open yourself to the new, the more of the old floods in with it. Our lives and our books are daisy-chains of anxieties and influences, second-hand impressions. You couldn't break that chain if you wanted to. And why would you want to? What good would it do? You'd wind up floating out there, remote and alone like Tavolara, the world's tiniest sovereign kingdom. No access, no bridges, no people.

Perhaps this is why, after ten days spent following the Lawrences across the island, we now feel an odd reluctance to say goodbye. We'll miss their hammering, contentious company. We'll miss the Q-B's shrewd, sanguine temperament, her relish for shopping and pricing. We may even miss her husband, old D. H. himself. That feverish kvetch with his endless litany of grievances, his bruised, enormous heart—Sardinia, at least for us, will be an infinitely duller story without his grumbling voice-over in our ears, the chryon of his complaints crawling below the picture.

Why *did* he come to these "unknown lands"? And what did he find? Only in retrospect does the answer begin to emerge, slowly taking on definition, like a photo in a chemical bath. "A nostalgia for something I know not what . . . a heart yearning for something I have known, and which I want back again." In the end, it seems to me, what Lawrence actually discovers in Sardinia is the same thing he discovers everywhere he goes. And it's not unknown at all. It's not pre-human; it's not pre-Christian; it's not even pre-European. It's hiding out there in plain sight the whole time. It's in the fields around Mandas, which resemble "the bleak parts of Cornwall." It's in Gavoi, which reminds him of the "sense of roving, as in an English countryside." It's north of Cagliari, in the "wide, almost Celtic landscape of hills." Lawrence in Sardinia is the oldest story in the world. For all his frantic wanderings, all his endless, peripatetic exile, he's like

Dorothy in Oz: he never really leaves home after all. Wherever the whirlwind takes him, it's all pretty much the same dream.

As for stony old Sardinia, it remains, for all our presumptions, untouched as ever, a big solitary rock in the center of the sea. The centuries come and go, the writers visit and leave, the cruise ships slog past on their way to Barcelona. Sardinia pays no attention. It just sits there, neither welcoming nor resisting interpretation. It is what it is. The judgment may be wrong but like the man said, that was the impression I got.

Kafka's Budget Guide to Florence

During a trip that they took together in August and September of 1911, Kafka and Max Brod hit on the idea of creating a new type of travel guide. "It would be called 'Billig' ('On the Cheap')," Brod remembered. "Franz was tireless and got a childlike pleasure out of elaborating all the principles down to the finest detail for this new type of guide, which was supposed to make us millionaires, and above all wrest us away from our awful office work."
—Reiner Stach, *Is That Kafka?*

Exploring Florence

Whoever leads a solitary life and yet now and then wishes to attach himself somewhere, anywhere—to be drawn at last, that is to say, into human relation, human harmony—might do well to come to Florence in the shoulder season, when the prices are lower and the narrow, crowded streets, with laborious effort and the proper shoes, can still be managed. There is so much to see. One chases after the city, stumbling and frantic, like a beginner learning to skate. And yet how can one be glad about the world unless one occasionally takes refuge in it?

There is no having, only a state of being that craves suffocation.

ORIENTATION

Arriving by train, one emerges into a vast, deserted terminal. The clocks may well be broken, the information kiosk shuttered and dark. The currency exchange, notwithstanding the numbers displayed in the window, inevitably leaves the visitor at some confusing and unaccountable deficit. It's comforting to believe that the disproportion of the world is merely arithmetical.

Outside the station, you will study the bus schedule in fastidious detail but find no comprehensive geography, only a number of highly specific routes that do not intersect.

There is a goal, but no way. The tourist's dilemma.

It is important, especially in high season, to book early. All human error is the result of impatience. The pension we recommend (*La Locanda Discutibile*) is a bit off the beaten path, in a quiet residential district on an unmarked street. The way is infinitely long. You must proceed by some vague, formless intuition, listening to the occasional ringing noise of your own footsteps on the cobblestones, which echoes faintly but continuously as you advance. Or *have* you advanced? Perhaps you have only traveled a circle.

Beyond a certain point there is no return; that is the point you must reach.

Upon arrival, take care to approach the desk clerk, as all figures of authority, with calmness and equanimity. Remember that were it not for his various familial and professional obligations, this poor minor official, hemmed in behind a desk burdened with meaningless paperwork, might prefer to be an idle visitor in a foreign country, too. Politely, and in your best Italian, explain that you have come a long way through an indeterminate landscape for reasons you find difficult to remember, let alone articulate, and that you would prefer a room away from the street noise, perhaps one with a pleasant view of the courtyard. The clerk will listen to you attentively, frowning and pulling at his moustache. Then, in the meekest, most solicitous and apologetic manner, he will decline to honor your reservation.

This is the Italian way. It is not necessary to accept it as just; one must only accept it as necessary.

FOOD AND DRINK

Though the adventurous tourist will rejoice in Florence's variety of excellent *ristoranti*, those who find it difficult to digest such rich, heavy food, or indeed any food at all, may struggle. Most local eating establishments close one or two days a week; some remain closed all seven. The *menus del giorno* are rarely legible from the street. The prices you will have to guess at, and you will invariably guess wrong.

Remember that you will be charged for the bread (*pane a coperto*) that appears automatically on your table when you sit down, despite the fact that you did not order it, do not want it, have no intention of eating it, and can scarcely bear to look at it. Why would you, when they use no salt? Nobody can desire what is ultimately damaging to him.

A note for the inexperienced traveler: the local pasta (*pappardelle alla lepre*) has been known to hit the stomach like a guillotine: as heavy, as light.

Most visitors to the city choose to start at the Cathedral—or the *Duomo* as they call it—as there is no avoiding the weight of its looming and magnificent shadow, which they experience as a kind of incitement, or goad. Naturally, the doors will be closed when you arrive. Peer in as best you can at the six side windows on the basilica, notable for their delicate tracery and ornaments (only the four closest to the transept admit light), and the wrought-iron candles affixed to the pillars—lovely but quite inadequate for illuminating the altarpieces in the side chapels. It is as if the candles have been put there to magnify the darkness that surrounds them.

One of the first signs of the beginnings of understanding is the wish to die.

Take advantage of the delay—for there are often delays, gaining entry into the Cathedral—to sample a panforte, the dense, nearly impenetrable Tuscan fruitcake, in a nearby café. Remember that a cake uneaten, regarded from its own point of view, is only a boring object made out of flour.

After a long morning of sightseeing, the visitor may wish to indulge in the Italian *siesta* and let a head filled with hate and disgust droop on the breast.

Late afternoons are best for the Uffizi Gallery, which draws hordes of visitors, most of them quite noisy and boorish, in every season. Try to avoid the tour groups with their piping, mousy docents. Remember that those who love other people are no more nor less unjust than those who love themselves; there remains only the question of whether the former is possible.

Across the Arno, the *Palazzo Pitti* offers a unique opportunity to view the regal home of the Medicis and their glorious collection of Titians, Raphaels, and Rubens. You may observe that some of the later rooms are more notable for their gaudy Empire furnishings and decorations than for the pictures themselves. One can't help but reflect upon the shallow philistinism of the rich, how much wealth they invest in an effort to insulate themselves from the sufferings of the world. And yet this insulation is the one form of suffering they might have avoided.

In the struggle between one's self and the world, bet on the world.

Traveling with Children

It is true that some children, separated from the comfort of their routines—perhaps their mother has inadvertently spoiled them—grow balky and sullen to the point of morbidity. One should seek to win them over with affection. On a hot afternoon, a kindly word from Father, a quiet taking by the hand, a friendly or encouraging look, might lend them the necessary confidence and well-being to go on searching through the winding streets near Santa Croce, hour after hour, looking for a gelato place a friend once told you about.

Telephones

The Florentine area code is 055. Most phones have six numbers, but don't be surprised if some have seven, four, or even eight. If you require assistance, dial "O," and wait for the operator. You will hear a rather vague and indistinct hum on the line, perhaps meaningful, perhaps not. As you go on waiting, remember that believing in progress and making progress are not the same thing. It is only your weakness, vanity, passivity, and lack of imagination that makes you cling to this notion of an "operator" in the first place.

Tipping

Service is generally included in all hotel and restaurant bills. However, many people find it customary to leave an additional gratuity. Those who leave a tip and those who don't leave a tip feel equally guilty and sinful, the first because they are only pretending to have free will in the matter, the second because they are failing even to pretend. The fact that there is nothing but a spiritual world deprives us of hope but gives us consolation.

Nightlife

Martyrs do not underrate the body; they allow it be elevated on the cross. As do, in their own way, the famous Florentine bordellos. Just saying!

Sadly, Florence is not free from petty crime. The best way to protect your valuables is to leave them at home. You should ask yourself if one really needs expensive jewelry or favorite heirlooms on a trip. You should ask yourself if one even needs to *go* on a trip. Perhaps upon reflection, no trip is necessary. Perhaps in the end it's better to stay home. To just sit at your writing table and listen. Or not even listen, just wait. Or not even wait, just sit there unmoving, quiet and alone, as the world writhes in raptures at your feet.

Might the most useful *Budget Travel* guide of all be the one that is never written, only conceived?

It is only in negation that things take on their true form.

Invisible Ink

A Mystery

On Sundays, like all dutiful sons with pretensions to virtue, I call my father. My father is ninety-four years old, a veteran of the conveyor business. Though rust has now corroded his energies his mind's motor grinds on, bearing a revolving freight of anxieties, irritations, and deflating remarks. "Still working on that novel?" he demanded recently, as he often does—as, let's face it, he always does.

"*Mpph*," I said, or some monosyllable to that effect.

"I only ask because I've been doing some math here, and it seems to be taking you a lot longer than it used to."

"Possibly so," I said. "Though you ask me about it a lot more than you used to, too."

"It just seems like a long time, that's all I'm saying. Doesn't it seem like a long time to you?"

"To be honest," I said, as I do when I'm not being honest, "it's never crossed my mind." Then I hung up, or rather pressed the phone face-down on my desk with both hands, like a lid below which all the rumbling Oedipal discontents of a lifetime boiled and hissed.

All things considered it was a pretty typical conversation with my father—and with me too, frankly. Nonetheless like most of our conversations it did not so much end when it was over as fester and swell like an unchecked infection in my head. Why *was* I writing so slowly, and in such invisible ink? When had that started? What did it mean? And most important, when and how would it *end*? Perhaps, on some level to which I lacked access, this was actually a good thing, I told myself, or in any case not a bad one. But whatever that level was, I couldn't find it. I couldn't access it.

So I began to look around for other levels instead. Other levels, and other models. Whether I did so for inspiration or instruction—or maybe just consolation—didn't matter. It was the looking that appealed to me. As long as I kept looking, the future seemed pliable to me, open-ended, expansive. It was the finding I dreaded. The dark knowledge that shuts things down for good.

"We lie down," writes Don Paterson, *"when the length of our shadows becomes intolerable."* The suggestive logic of this mordant little epigram seems almost tautological. I like the sneaky reverse-engineering of its syntax: the movement from action (or its failure) to depletion to weary, self-lacerating judgment. Here is the writer at the end of the day, struggling to keep him/herself vertical. Top-heavy lies the crown, when it sits on that huge, clogged-up head, crusty and sodden with old impressions. It's like a used coffee filter: not much gets through. A lugubrious trickle. A slow, attenuated drip. Even a writer as muscular and propulsive as Conrad knew the taste of that acrid brew:

> I never mean to be slow. The stuff comes out at its own rate. . . . I seem to have lost all sense of style and yet I am haunted by the necessity of style. And that story I can't write weaves itself into all I see . . . I feel my brain. I am distinctly conscious of the contents of my head. My story is there in a fluid—in an evading shape. I can't get hold of it . . . any more than you can grasp a handful of water.

"I am distinctly conscious of the contents of my head." Writers and neurotics everywhere—presuming these are two different categories—can identify all too well with the desperation and the lucidity of this *cri de coeur*: the creative mind under assault by its own profusions, its own largely self-generated phantoms. Desperation is an unreliable fuel source; it burns out quickly, and doesn't always move you forward. But suppose burning out for some people is a *way* of moving forward, that a writer is at their best and most free when they're at their worst and most stuck. The usual exits blocked, the usual fluencies and facilities stymied. Might that account for how much great writing has been done over the years about the impossibility of great writing? How much verbal intensity has been achieved by cataloguing the failures of language to do any justice to the reality of experience at all?

Take the narrator, if you can call him that, of Beckett's *Unnameable*:

> *They're (the words) going to stop, I know that well: I can feel it. They're going to abandon me. It will be the silence, for a moment (a good few moments). Or it will be mine? The lasting one, that didn't last, that still lasts?*

Or Artaud:

I am suffering from a frightful malady of the mind, a kind of erosion. My thoughts evade me in every way possible. There is something that is destroying my thinking, something that does not prevent me from being what I might be, but which leaves me in abeyance; a something furtive which takes away the words I have found . . . which diminishes my intensity, which takes away from me even the memory of the devices and figures of speech by which one expresses oneself.

Or Flaubert:

You don't know what it is to stay a whole day with your head in your hands trying to squeeze your unfortunate brain so as to find a word. Ideas come very easily with you, incessantly, like a stream. With me it is a tiny thread of water.

Or Kafka:

7 February. Complete standstill. Unending torments.

You get the idea. After a few of these florid complaints, your gentle reader has doubtless had her fill. Who can blame her? There's something more than a little indulgent in them, the relish of a child picking at a scab. If Einstein is right that a problem can't be solved with the same tools and at the same level of consciousness that created it, why try?

Possibly the best solution for that over-clogged filter of ours, in short, is to just give it a rest. Put it away for a while. Stop pouring in words and thoughts. Just, you know, shut the fuck up.

In *Silence: The Phenomenon and Its Ontological Significance*, Bernard P. Dauenhauer laments the failure of artistic discourse to capture a universe "unencompassable in discourse." He describes a process of unfolding, a "fore-and-after silence" that allows space for evolution of expression. We see this same impulse in Emerson: "Let us be silent, for so are the gods. Silence is a solvent that destroys personality." For Emerson, a kind of homegrown Buddhist, the destruction of personality is something to be encouraged. And who would argue with that? What strong personality doesn't secretly wish to be relieved of itself?

So maybe that's the answer. A little constructive silence. An interlude of retreat. Enough with the digging and sifting like a gold-miner, trying to unearth the world's treasures. Enough with the forging in the smithy of one's soul. Maybe just *chill out*. Take some instruction from Pablo Neruda's poem, "Keeping Quiet":

> Now we will count to twelve
> and we will all keep still
> for once on the face of the earth,
> let's not speak in any language;
> let's stop for a second,
> and not move our arms so much.
> It would be an exotic moment without rush, without engines;
> we would all be together
> in a sudden strangeness.

Maybe so. Though I doubt it. To my nose this poem, and the sentiment behind it, carries a slight whiff of perfume. Like patchouli, a little goes a long way. Pretty as it is to think so, most of us are incapable of sitting still around the campfire, counting mindfully to twelve. We prefer life in the other camp, the noisy, lit-up side of the lake. There's no *time* over there to sit around; there's too many books to write, too much status and money to hunter-gather, too many resentments and grievances to compile. Maybe, we think, if our engines are going to shut down at some point anyway, we should go ahead and use them while we still can. Better to keep slogging down that twisted Via Dolorosa called a literary career, bearing our crosses, than to pull over and snooze. After all it's the road—the life—we've chosen. No one forced us to do it. So why complain? As my father, that tireless pundit, is forever calling to remind me, *These are the jokes, so you better start laughing.*

And indeed it *can* be funny, the flailings of the long distance writer, struggling to stay afloat atop an ocean of turbulent silence. Is that waving, or drowning? Who can tell? ("Man possesses four things that are no good at sea," Machado tells us. "Anchor, rudder, oars, and the fear of going down.") But that same fear bears us up, too. That fear keeps us going—blindly, unthinkingly, mechanically—makes us carry on with our writing as a drowning person might be said to carry on with their swimming: because it's the only way we know of to stay alive.

Or maybe that's too grand a statement. Maybe it's just business, a professional thing. When you're a pro, you're supposed to go on being a pro all the way. And a pro shows up for work. "A professional makes the pot boil," says Henry James, "it's the only basis of sanity and freedom." Never mind that his own meals were insanely elaborate affairs, full of bedazzling tasting menus and finicky triple-jointed feats of molecular gastronomy. At heart poor Henry is just another fry cook, churning out the specials, or so he'd have us think. Anyway the point stands: if you want to call yourself a working artist, you have to go on working, being artistic. Even if, in the wrong hands, the former comes at the expense of the latter.

James's own hands, it goes without saying, were fully capable of juggling both. But then he wasn't just a pro, but a Master, a consummate practitioner of an arcane, demanding craft. But say you're not a Master. Say you're just gifted. Say you're just gifted and driven and vain enough to have successfully convinced yourself you *may* be a Master someday. Say that you feel, by virtue of your gift and drive and vanity, that you are one of the Chosen, summoned to your vocation's altar and bestowed with a sacred scroll, crowned with gold, where the mythos of life on earth is latently inscribed, waiting to be incanted into song. Surely that would help keep you peppy and productive. As for the rest of us, we have to go on muddling along as best we can. Not everyone can be the Chosen, after all. The numbers don't pan out. There's no meaning to being the Chosen if there isn't a much larger body of the Not-Chosen to be Chosen *from*. That's how it works.

But writing of course is not a gift. If it *were* a gift, it would be no big deal to misplace it, or return it, or even casually throw it away. But writing, it gives me no pleasure to report, is a job. Plodding, methodical, even borderline bourgeois. The stability it requires, the quotidian habits and routines, the tolerance for that boring, humdrum labor of making something out of nothing, laying one sentence down after another ("*Like a donut-maker*," in DeLillo's famous phrase, "*only slower*") atop an invisible and unstable foundation—none of this is cool or glamorous. Any romantic edge it might offer quickly wears away under the rasp of repetition. All that's left is the writing itself. That's the bottom line. The writer, simply speaking, is someone who writes. The rest is commentary.

This becomes all too clear by the way when one stops writing for a while, and then resumes. "When I begin to write after a long interval," Kafka notes in his diary, "I draw the words as if out of the empty air. If I capture one, then I have just this one alone, and all the toil must begin anew." We'd like to think that writing, like riding a bicycle, is a muscle memory that can't be forgotten. But it's more like *reconditioning* a bicycle. It takes a ludicrous amount of time, effort, and elbow grease, and meanwhile you're stuck in the garage all day, tinkering with recalcitrant gears. No sun on your face, no wind in your hair, no downhill exhilaration. You feel like you may never get back on the road. You're no longer even sure you want to. Your concentration and rage for speed have gone AWOL; your core hungers, the psychic wounds that have driven you forward, have mysteriously dried up, the scabs peeling away, leaving only the faintest of scars, stubbornly imprinted, like a terminal sentence in your own private penal colony.

Kafka himself understood this feeling all too well, if this short piece of his is any indication:

I can swim as well as the others, only I have a better memory than they do, so I have been unable to forget my formerly not being able to swim. Since I have been unable to forget it, being able to swim doesn't help me, and I can't swim after all.

The narrator here, like Borges's Funes the Memorious, suffers a paralyzing surfeit of consciousness, one that paradoxically renders him incapable of doing what he knows he's perfectly capable of doing. Perhaps on some level he prefers not to swim, but if so, he's unaware of it. All he knows is he can't. His ability to swim has slowed not just to a crawl, as it were, but a stop. In other words, his memory of swimming has been lapped so decisively by his memory of not-swimming that the appeal of swimming and/or not-swimming is more or less exhausted. Now he's content, or anyway resigned, just to hang out by the side of the pool, reflecting on his own absence from the water—a vacancy that calls attention, as vacancies do, to what should be there, but isn't. It reminds me of a line I read once in the diaries of another finicky, impacted Jewish writer: *"I've written little because there is so much not to be said."*

Dave Chappelle, asked about his choice to disappear at the very height of his fame, replied: "It makes no sense at all. There's nothing anyone can say. It's just you do what you feel like you need to do."

None of which applies, really, when you're young and spry, just starting out. When you're young and spry and just starting out, you tend to gaze out over the vocational landscape and see only the battles won: triumphant generals leading crisp, orderly columns, swords gleaming in the light. But after you've endured a few wars yourself, you may begin to view things differently, training your binoculars around the margins of the battlefield, toting up the casualties and deserters, the wounded and missing along the way. It turns out to be quite a list. Here you thought God was on *your* side; so why does he so often show up in the enemy's uniform?

The women, as always, suffer worst in this war, laying down arms to keep home and hearth going, in ways Tillie Olsen, Virginia Woolf, Natalia Ginzburg, and countless others have fiercely and thoroughly documented. But the men don't fare so great either. Some go broke, some get sick, some are lost in the woods, some go into hiding, some get hooked on anesthetizing drugs. Some can't find the time to write, some find the time but not the words, some start things but don't finish them, some finish things but can't start them, some start and finish things but can't or won't publish them. True, everyone starts out with some degree of promise ("Whom the gods wish to destroy," wrote Cyril Connolly, "they first call promising"), but a good number start coasting after a while, and then gradually age out of the business. Some outgrow their own material. Some get weary of their own little moves. Some lose all tolerance for anxiety and isolation. Some, the opportunists, turn their losses into commodities, make a lucrative fetish of their own defeats.

And then there are the purists. The refuseniks. The *No, in Thunder!* types who turn their backs on the whole business, and take up other, more wholesome pursuits. They may breed ducks up in Maine, à la Henry Roth; vanish into the jungles of Mexico, à la B. Traven; run coffee and guns in a the Horn of Africa, à la Rimbaud. ("*I can now say art is an idiocy*," he's said to have declared, on his way out the door.)

Finally there are those who are none of the above. Those who for one reason or another, or sometimes no reason at all, simply get off the train one day at the local stop, and don't get back on. It might not be a decision, just a vague, transient impulse: a mood, a daydream, a cloud that drifts by and momentarily occludes the sun. Without any particular intention, they may go meandering off into the terminal, buy a sandwich or a cup of coffee, and then meander back in time to see the train pulling away without them, with no evident friction or resistance. They watch it go. What they feel in that moment is mysterious. It's not panic exactly, neither is it exhilaration; it's more like some third, weirdly pacific emotion for which I'm tempted to say no word exists. Except the Germans, who have a word for everything, have a word for it. They call it *gelassenheit*, or "releasement."

We see this word popping up here and there in German philosophy. Heidegger for one uses it a lot. It's hard to say precisely what he means by it—or let's face it, by anything really—but it seems to be an impulse to move away or be delivered from the linear noise of "calculative thought," toward an inward sphere of paradox, mystery, and things-as-they-are-ness he calls "meditative thought." (The Zen masters, as usual, got there first:

"*That which is before you is it*," writes Huang Po, "*Begin to reason about it and you at once fall into error*.") And who among us would argue with that?

What's less clear is what happens *after* this releasement of his. Say we are released too well, from too much, for too long. Say the intuitive dream *refuses to end*, but meanders on and on and on as we stand there frozen on the platform watching trains pull in and out, never going anywhere at all. Say our releasement, in short, turns out to be yet another cage. How do we release ourselves from *that*?

Consider the case of Hawthorne's "Wakefield," a man who one day walks out of his house with no forethought or explanation, abandons his wife and children, and takes up secret residence a few blocks away, where he remains for the next twenty years. Twenty years! How's *that* for *gelassenheit*! Wakefield's magic act, this existential escape of his, wriggling free from the ties that bind, is the stuff of a family man's dreams—and nightmares too. Like Rip Van Winkle, in transcending his routines he has entered a lonely, haunting orbit from which it's not clear he can ever return. How strong *are* the ties that bind us to the world, if they can be snapped so easily, so whimsically? "By stepping aside for a moment," the story concludes, "a man exposes himself to a fearful risk of losing his place forever . . . he may become, as it were, The Outcast of the Universe." You can almost hear Rod Serling's voice intoning these words, wrapping up a particularly chilling episode of *The Twilight Zone*.

And yet this same note can be heard reverberating through countless works of literature and in the lives of those who wrote them. Melville and Hardy, Ellison and Salinger and Kesey, Katherine Ann Porter and Bette Howland and Lucia Berlin; Vila-Matas and Juan Rulfo; Fitzgerald and Hammett, B. Traven and Joseph Mitchell . . . all depict in their work and/ or manifest in their lives the same Wakefield-ian spirit of self-exile. It seems this urge to step away from the vehicle is more common than we think. The occupational hazard all artists face is that in spending your life making something out of nothing, there may come a day when the nothing wins. When you look down and discover you're not the agile Road Runner but poor Wile E. Coyote, with no solid ground under your feet. And then whoops, here it comes, gravity's sickening plunge . . .

All of which may leave you feeling a bit nervous and hesitant as you go forward—if you *do* go forward—subjecting every word you write to more scrutiny than words can bear. Hopefully you don't become disabled by it. A lot of people do. Take Robert Walser, for example, the great hyper-neurotic Swiss writer who spent his last three decades in a mental hospital. "I'm not here to write," he declared upon entry, "I'm here to be mad." Whether he said this with resignation or relief isn't clear.

Walser was one of those writers whose loss of traction seems inevitable in retrospect. Writing was *literally* difficult for him. He disdained the typewriter, and wrote instead in a fastidious, labor-intensive hand. That hand began to seize up in his thirties, suffering crippling, possibly psychosomatic cramps which he attributed, like all good *Mittel-europeans*, to his Unconscious. In short, he believed his hand was expressing a latent, vicious animus toward his pen. Crazy as this sounds, he might have been right: it was only after he switched to a pencil that he managed to eke out a few words a day again.

The seeds of this antagonism can be seen poking through the crust of an early Walser story, "Kleist in Thun," in which authorial projection is almost comically transparent. Anyone who's logged time in an artist's colony will recognize the predicament: Kleist, our writer-hero, having retreated to the countryside to get some work done, is now blessed with ideal conditions for that very task. The fields are thick with flowers, the bees hum drowsily overhead, the intoxicating fragrances of summer fill up every room. And yet when he sits down to write nothing happens. Nada. Zip. Every word makes him grimace; every stab at creation miscarries; and meanwhile the weeks pass, the tension accumulates, the resolve to write—and not just any old shit by the way, but something brilliant and original and significant, to redeem all these weeks of futility—grows and grows. Anyone care to guess how *that* works out?

"Weeks pass, Kleist has destroyed one work, two, three works. He wants the highest mastery, good, good. What's that? Not sure? Tear it up. Something new, wilder, more beautiful." The hunger for perfection has grown so unappeasable, so bottomless, it more or less guarantees the futility of writing anything at all. That Walser would, in his own life, succumb to just such a fit of despair a few years later (even his suicide attempt was aborted because, he said, "I couldn't even make a proper noose") seems almost overdetermined: the closing of a circle that was never, in fact, open.

Let's console ourselves with the recognition that the Walsers of the world are outliers. Most writers are not Walsers. (Enrique Vila-Matas in his own brilliant meditation on the subject, *Bartleby & Co*, argues that even *Walser* wasn't a Walser, as he never lost sight of the fact that "writing that one cannot write is also writing.") Not to say that our facility and confidence will blithely override all obstacles. Not to say that we never have occasion to doubt ourselves. Not to say that we never experience a vertiginous disconnect between words and feeling, a bleak conviction that language can't free us from the labyrinth of consciousness, but can only take us further in. But fine. Let's accept that words are just manmade tools that separate us from nature behind walls of our own construction. So what? As Popeye used to say, *dem's de conditions dat obtain*. In the end, it's not that complicated. Most of us go on writing for the simplest, most persuasive of reasons: because we can't find anything else to do.

Hugo von Hoffmanstahl's *Letter of Lord Chandos* (1902) reads, on the surface, as yet another haunting, Walser-like account of a writer losing his sense of traction, purpose, and coherence. All the familiar signs of breakdown are here, swirling around like so much frenzied static on a too-bright screen:

> I no longer succeeded in comprehending . . . with the simplifying eye of habit. For me everything disintegrated into parts; . . . single words floated round me; they congealed into eyes which stared at me and into which I was forced to stare back—whirlpools which gave me vertigo and, reeling incessantly, led into the void.

Ironically, what emerges from this epic breakdown is a break*through* for Hoffmanstahl himself, who, even as he sinks to the bottom of his own well of faith, has the presence of mind to take notes along the way. Turning the weight of his own inertia upside down, he manages to transform his descent into an ascent. A sneaky inversion. A kind of austere martial art. And isn't that the best-case scenario for any creative person—to plunge deep into the jungle of self, and emerge from that thronged, suffocating darkness with a travel journal, full of visceral details and haunting atmosphere, from which to draw material and inspiration and maybe even a few penetrating insights going forward? Even Walser, for all his claims of having stopped writing altogether, left five hundred pages behind after his death—inscribed in a microscopic, nearly illegible pencil script—which is believed to be a diary in secret code.

Stepping off the train, in other words, is not the same as not moving. It may simply mean you're opening yourself to alternate destinations, other forms of transport. For Hoffmanstahl, the struggle to renounce and withdraw from all literary achievement paradoxically led to an achievement so *sui generis* as to vault clear over modernism's runway and out into the bleak, stripped-down landscape beyond. We recognize the look of that place now, because we've all been there with Beckett. The bare stage, the muttering head trying to talk its way into a silence it can't find. If it's even findable. "No silence exists that is not pregnant with sound," says John Cage. Who should know.

So forget silence. We can chase it all we like, we're never going to catch up. And even we did we'd probably regret it, as a dog regrets catching up to a car. Maybe the chase itself will have to do. Or maybe not chasing anything for a while, just hovering for a while in a state of attention, suspension, reception. Practicing a kind of writing that acknowledges the possibility, perhaps even the appeal, of not writing at all. "*An affirmation, I mean negation,*" Beckett calls it, "*on which to build.*"

⌒∞⌒

It probably goes without saying that it took me forever to write this essay, the last in a book of essays I was putting together. True, each one of them seemed, as I wrote them, to take forever. And yet in retrospect I wrote the others much more quickly than this one, which really *did* seem to take forever. I'd like to think this means the next essay I write will make this one seem in retrospect to have not taken forever after all. But more likely it means I will stop writing essays for a while, period.

In any case, when I finally I finished that book—that is, this book—I called my father and told him.

There was a pause. I could hear the harsh, grating sound he makes when he clears his throat, whether in a rhetorical way or because his throat is perpetually clogged, who knows. "So what about the book?" he asked.

My father's memory not being what it was, I tried to keep my voice level. "I just told you about the book."

"I mean the other book," he said. "The novel."

"Oh. Well, what about it?"

"Is it done? Because I've been doing the math, and it's been a long time now. Aren't you working on it?"

"Yeah."

"It's funny," he said, "how you say you're working, but it never seems to get done. Why do you think that is?"

Robert Cohen's books include the novels *Inspired Sleep, Amateur Barbarians, The Here and Now*, and *The Organ Builder*, as well as a collection of short fiction, *The Varieties of Romantic Experience*. Among his awards are fellowships from the Guggenheim Foundation, the Whiting Foundation, the Lila-Wallace Reader's Digest Foundation, and a Pushcart Prize. He has taught fiction writing and literature at Harvard University, the Iowa Writers Workshop, the University of Houston, and the Warren Wilson MFA Program for Writers. He currently teaches at Middlebury College.

Printed and bound by CPI Group (UK) Ltd, Croydon, CR0 4YY

09/06/2025

14685673-0001